WHAT THEY DON'T TEACH YOU IN MEDICAL & DENTAL SCHOOL

360° Approach to Financial Planning and Practice Management

Farid Mokhtarian, CLTC, RFC, C(k)P

Ata Walizadeh, RFC, Ph.D.

WHAT THEY DON'T
TEACH YOU IN
MEDICAL & DENTAL SCHOOL

Copyright © 2016
Farid Mokhtarian, CLTC, RFC, C(k)P
Ata Walizadeh, RFC, Ph.D.
LCCN 2016937102

ISBN 978-0-692-73982-2

Printed in the United States of America
1 3 5 7 9 10 8 6 4 2

ACKNOWLEDGMENTS

WE WOULD LIKE TO THANK OUR SPOUSES, Kim Mokhtarian and Nahid Walizadeh. We couldn't have written this book without your patience, support, and love. In addition, we want to acknowledge our many clients who have worked with us through the years. The experiences we have shared with you, and the trust you have invested in us, has been more rewarding than we can ever express. Finally, we want to convey our appreciation to the readers of this book, for welcoming our ideas into your lives. We welcome you as well, and wish you much success and happiness!

SECURITIES OFFERED THROUGH THE LEADERS GROUP, INC. , MEMBER FINRA/SIPC, WWW.FINRA.ORG 26 WEST DRY CREEK CIRCLE, SUITE 575, LITTLETON, CO. 80120 (303) 797-9080. PHYSICIANS PENSION & INSURANCE SER-VICES (DBA), AND S.R.S BUSINESS AND PERSONAL INSURANCE SERVICES, INC., ARE NOT AFFILIATED WITH THE LEADERS GROUP, INC. ATA WALIZADEH & FARID MOKHTARIAN ARE REGISTERED REPRESENTATIVES. CALIFORNIA INSURANCE LICENSE # 0H18237

CONTENTS

PART ONE
INTRODUCTION

Chapter 1

WHAT IS A FINANCIAL PLAN?

THIS IS A BOOK FOR PHYSICIANS. While financial planning is important for every individual and business owner, it is a particularly big topic for physicians, and particularly now. Changes in the American health care system are happening with astonishing speed, and their effects on the way doctors practice medicine and run their businesses cannot be ignored. There is much uncertainty about the details of the changes health care reform will bring, but there is no doubt that doctors are in the center of a rapidly changing world. Shifts from a traditional "fee for service" model of payments for medical care to global payments and risk contracts will bring a fundamental shift in the way doctors earn income, and—more importantly—in the predictability and security of these income streams. Large institutions, like government agencies and insurance companies, will play increasingly important roles in controlling these income streams through rate-setting, approval of payments to providers, and the establishment of new networks of providers serving geographic and demographic groups. It's enough to confuse and confound even the most business-savvy physician, or to distract any doctor from the primary purpose of the medical profession: seeing and taking care of patients.

This book will help physicians focus on some of the important steps they can take in managing their finances, including the income streams from the services they provide and the assets they use in delivering care, or own by themselves or with their families outside of work. We'll look at these strategies and concepts in three important areas: first, as physicians; second, as owners of the small businesses where they see patients; and third, as individuals and members of a family. In each case, regardless of changes brought about by health care reform or other outside forces, there are basic concepts around which a successful financial plan can always be built. A book like this one, written by experienced financial planners, contains a number of "constants" that are relevant even in a world defined by change. In fact, these concepts are designed specifically for managing one's way through a constantly changing world. If you are looking for specific "rules" to apply in a particular set of circumstances, or at a particular stage of a career, or in response to a particular event in your business, this is not the book for you.

In fact, neither are the books that do lay out a neat series of rules, with guidelines on when to apply them. The truth is that the future is always uncertain, and financial planning rules are often unreliable. One or two small deviations in a situation that looks a lot like the environment where these rules worked well in the past can make the difference between continued success in applying these rules and financial ruin. Instead of providing readers with a general set of rules and when to apply them, this book will introduce and explain powerful financial concepts, tools, and resources that can be studied for their potential, and matched to the unique and real circumstances of a physician's professional, business, and personal worlds. These concepts have been proven to maximize income, and to protect assets once they're owned, but only in the context of being the right tools at the right time. Information about the advantages and disadvantages of these tools and resources are included, to help a physician add his or her own judgment to prepare for the uncertain world everyone faces when starting a financial plan. And finally, even though it may sound like a self-serving thing for a financial advisor to say, we highly recommend finding—or keeping—a financial advisor you trust, so that you can discuss the concepts laid out in this book and maximize their value. Physicians understand the value of specialized knowledge; they use it every day in helping patients live longer, healthier lives. Financial advisors have a similarly specialized knowledge base that helps their clients live more secure and rewarding lives—lives that are made more secure and rewarding through strategies that increase income potential and protect the assets a successful physician will acquire during his or her career.

Before getting into the concepts we will introduce in this book, one final point about the similarities between physicians and their world of health management, and financial advisors and our world of financial management. Today's health care system is committed to engaging each individual in managing his or her health. Improved nutrition and exercise, education about habits to adopt or avoid to stay healthy, self-administration of prescription medications, and even self-management of chronic conditions like diabetes or high blood pressure are all part of what doctors call "patient-centered care." Physicians can provide education and guidance for their patients in how to take many of these steps on their own, reducing possible acute conditions that would require emergency care or hospitalization. Similarly, financial advisors can teach individuals similar basic skills to manage their own financial "health," applying tools like insurance protection, compliance with government regulations, business organization strategies, and retirement planning in their daily lives. These concepts can also keep the finances of individuals and families more stable and secure, reducing the risk of crises that might require drastic action. But, just as a doctor is always ready to help in an emergency, a financial advisor can also play a similar role for his or her clients, standing ready to provide specific advice when unique situations—good or bad—occur. So read on, learn, and apply the financial planning tools and concepts you'll find in subsequent chapters of this book. But please consider our recommendation that you find and keep a trusted financial advisor as the first lesson we can offer. You may not understand the value of this lesson every day, but when the time comes, there can be no better financial planning resource. We promise.

Like all individuals, physicians need basic information on investments, various types of insurance coverage, tax advice, retirement planning, and the new realities of health care reform for themselves and their families. While many physicians are likely to find themselves in the lucky company of other high-wealth individuals, physicians who are employed by a hospital or other health care institution and collect a salary—even a relatively large one—are not substantially different from other individuals looking for advice in how to manage their money. Their higher net worth might lead to more sophisticated strategies and investment "products" than others with fewer assets or lower incomes, but the fundamentals are similar with other highly-salaried, high-net-worth employees.

Note that throughout this book, we will tell stories about interactions between ourselves and other financial advisors and clients presenting "real" issues about their lives, financial situations, and concerns about the proper way to structure a successful financial plan. In all cases—and let us repeat, IN ALL CASES—these are fictional accounts based on our general experience in helping literally thousands of individuals. None of the people described in this book are real individuals; they are simply characters we have invented as a way for us to convey some of the ideas we want to share with you, our readers, in a way that illustrates the conversational nature of how financial planners and our clients interact. We are and always will be committed to respect for our clients and their families, and we take their confidentiality very seriously.

Part One of this book, including Chapters 1 and 2, is a general introduction to the concepts of financial planning, and why physicians need such a plan. In a way, the points we raise in these first chapters mirror the early conversations we have with many of our clients, particularly those who come to us as they take the first steps in creating their own financial plans. But even for physicians who have significant experience with financial planning—and perhaps with professional financial planners—we believe our ideas are worth considering if for no other reason than to introduce the way we approach the challenges that must be addressed in developing a successful financial plan. Sometimes it is more about the way we think than the specific thoughts we have that can shed light on the important concepts and considerations we hold most dear, and want to share most fully with the readers of this book.

Part Two, which includes Chapters 3, 4, and 5, is written to address the unique issues that make physicians' financial and practice management strategies so complex. HIPAA patient confidentiality requirements and the associated financial liability risks, doctors' legal responsibilities in the event of cyber attacks on electronic medical records, and the need to protect high-value medical equipment through additional insurance coverage are introduced in this section. Also introduced are creative business ideas like self-insurance or innovative incorporation models and buy-sell agreements to protect individual finances in the event of unplanned changes in ownership of a medical practice partnership or other business entity. Advice in how to manage the daily operation of a medical practice in a way that considers the needs and interests of patients is also offered here through the introduction of concepts such as psychological factors; leadership and management; kinesthetic body language; and marketing and public reviews. Finally, we will explore some of the current and pending changes flowing from health care reform, such as payment streams from state vs. federal exchanges and private insurers vs. government programs; and creative ways for managing uncertainty in a world where everything is different. The Affordable Care Act (ACA) affects physicians in a way it affects no other Americans: it makes changes to the income streams on which physicians have relied for decades. What does the change from fee-for-service to global payments mean? How much of a doctor's financial world will change, and how much will remain the same? Where are possible gaps in coverage and payments to physicians in new insurance networks and contracting procedures? How can physicians adjust their personal financial and practice management strategies to make the best of this new world?

Part Three, which includes Chapters 6, 7, and 8, includes financial and business management advice for small business owners; topics such as general liability insurance, workers' compensation, professional liability, business interruption insurance, and buy-sell agreements for co-owners and business partners are covered, along with the employee benefits and human resource issues every small business owner must face on a daily basis. Again, while no book can replace the real-time advantages of working with one's own financial advisor, we have gone to great efforts in making the contents of this book as current as possible as it goes to press.

Physicians who own and operate their own practices are small business owners, and as such can benefit from much of the content included in Part Three. Physicians who manage their own practices need guidance in how to manage what is essentially a small business. They need to understand government regulations that set boundaries on their operations, on a federal, state, and local level. They must protect their assets against uncertainties like fire and natural disasters, or lawsuits and litigation. Employee management and compensation must comply with regulations about workers' compensation, health insurance, and other benefits that may be required. Other optional employee benefits, such as retirement plans or 401(k) programs, must still comply with government regulations if they are implemented. Physicians who own or manage their own practices can find most of the answers they seek for their financial and business management in the same places other individuals or small business owners look for this information—including this book.

But physicians also face different small business management challenges. Their need for financial advice begins with general information that best serves individual employees or small business owners, but then it goes beyond these generalities in several ways. First, they need more, and different kinds of insurance. Their professional liability insurance goes beyond the typical "errors and omissions" type of coverage many small business owners require, and certainly far beyond the "umbrella" coverage many employed individuals purchase to cover their home and other personal assets. Physicians need malpractice insurance, and have for many years. Second, physicians often hold multiple positions in their careers at the same time. They may be employed by a hospital while also owning or co-owning their own practices, and they may also serve on the faculty of a medical school or other academic institution. Managing multiple income streams is not completely unusual among people in other professions, but it is particularly common for medical providers. And third, while physicians may be uniquely positioned with respect to health care reform and its effects on their income streams, as small business owners, they are also subject to its new requirements for providing employees with coverage in the same way all other small business owners are. Whether you call it Obamacare, or the Patient Protection and Affordable Care Act (its more formal name), this change in the delivery of American health care affects physicians in all three aspects of their financial planning: (1) as physicians who may see shifts in their income streams move from traditional "fee for service" payments to capitation, or risk contracts, (2) as small business owners who may be required to offer health insurance to their employees, and (3) as individual consumers of health insurance. As noted earlier in this introduction, information that is strictly defined within the management of a physician's practice is included in Part Two; advice for physicians that is related to their identity as small business owners can be found in Part Three; and a review of personal financial plans that apply to a physician and his family are listed in Part Four.

Part Four, which includes Chapters 9, 10, 11, and 12, provides detailed latest information about personal insurance, investment strategies, and retirement planning. These are important topics to be sure, and the advantage of reading a book written by experienced financial planners is our familiarity with both tried-and-true best practices for personal financial management, plus the constant attention we pay to changes that can alter these best practices in a relatively short time.

Taken as a whole, this book will seek to answer the question, "What should I (a physician) do?" in each of the chapters that follow. We will describe the situations in which financial and practice management advice might be helpful in detail but in plain language, and we will illustrate a few of the more interesting cases with real-life stories from physicians among the many clients who trust us to help them manage their personal, business management, and practice-specific finances. As is always the case, not all of the specific recommendations in this book will apply to every physician; each practice is always unique, and requires individualized attention in order to maximize its potential for success. Just as the work of being a professional financial advisor requires a "one size fits all" approach, being the author of a book about financial managers for physicians requires this same approach. We have already stated our reluctance to set out a list of rules that, if followed, will lead to success. Providing general principles for managing finances—first as a physician, second as a small business owner, and finally as an individual, is our primary goal in writing this book. Close behind is our next goal of communicating a broad conceptual understanding of the challenges and opportunities that come with the decision to go into the health care business. A third goal is a general principle behind all financial advice: always be prepared for the unexpected. Change is a part of life, and it is even more a part of running a successful business. Doctors practicing medicine fifty years ago would be astonished to find the way medicine is practiced in the modern world, and would be even more surprised to learn of the need for doctors to engage in many of the business practices we take for granted as part of practicing medicine in the early part of the twenty-first century. No doubt doctors fifty years from now will be similarly astonished to discover all of the primitive approaches we currently see as state-of-the-art. Their business practices may be even less comprehensible to us as ours would be to the doctors making house calls of yesteryear. In this way, our challenge is to open doctors' minds to the realities of an industry that is one of the largest segments of the American economy, and to prepare them for making decisions in this large and rapidly-changing world. If we accomplish these two goals, writing this book will be its own success story.

If you are a physician, welcome to a book we believe you will find very valuable in achieving success and maintaining financial security for yourself, your business, and your family. If you are not a physician but admire the work they do to keep us all healthy, share this book with a doctor you know and love. Return the favor of all he or she does to help us all. In either case, it's an investment that promises high returns.

Chapter 2

WHY PHYSICIANS NEED A FINANCIAL PLAN

"A good leader takes people to where they want to go. A great
leader takes people to where they ought to be."
~ Rosalynn Carter

REGARDLESS OF THEIR PROFESSION, most people have no finan-
cial plan at all; they just live day-to-day. This is true at all income levels,
and of course, the higher that level, the greater the risk of loss without a
plan. People making substantial amounts of money often spend impulsive-
ly, assuming that today's paychecks will go on forever, or even increase
over time. Those who think of investing for the future may do so in a
slightly less haphazard way, buying stocks based on stories in newspaper
financial pages or cable television business shows, or listening to stories
about friends' and family members' latest success in the market, or real estate, or other opportunities. Small business owners may be overwhelmed

by the growing demands for annual, quarterly, or even monthly reporting requirements for taxes, employee benefits, and other business activities, and as a result focus on simple compliance without weighing options for managing their way through these challenges to minimize costs and maximize the protection of their assets. Physicians can hardly get through a day without discovering "news" about some new opportunity brought about by health care reform, or a looming financial disaster they must address immediately before it destroys their practice.

Having no plan at all is bad enough, but haphazard "planning" that is nothing more than a series of knee-jerk reactions to unfiltered incoming information can be worse. At the very least, this is a common mistake. Financial planning begins by taking stock of our own situation. Risky investments may be acceptable for a young single physician, but they're not as advisable for an older doctor who has accumulated sizable assets and is thinking about retirement and estate planning for his family. But remember that not every aspect of a financial plan can be expressed in dollars and cents alone. Financial plans must support the life goals of an individual, and the goals he or she shares with family members. For example, traveling the world may be one individual's primary life goal, while it may not interest another person at all. Some parents believe strongly in providing their children with a college education, while other parents believe this is the responsibility of their children. These non-financial life goals must be considered when an individual embarks on the creation of a financial plan; plans that aren't based on considerations like these are incomplete. Similarly, financial plans are personal, and require careful attention to what is most important by the individual planner and his or her immediate family. It's important to avoid being distracted by "helpful" advice from friends and other family members. Your brother-in-law may have made a killing on a hot Chinese stock last month, but, as compelling as this story might be, it's not relevant to the development of a carefully designed, personalized financial plan that is right for *you*.

These personalized considerations aren't limited to individual and family realities alone. They also must be considered in our professional lives. Some people enjoy the independence of running their own businesses and find freedom in entrepreneurship. Others like being part of a large organization that provides security, and relish a different kind of freedom this choice brings—freedom from the responsibilities for employee management, compliance with regulations, and managing risk. This particular point is worth contemplating. Simply saying that "freedom" is an important part of our life goals isn't enough. What kind of freedom do we value? The same can be said about security, wealth, happiness, and other words that can mean very different things for every individual. Because this is a book about financial planning and practice management for physicians, we won't go into details about what different people may think about goals like freedom, security, and happiness. But we will focus on one important distinction between people we believe is essential. There are people who plan, and there are people who don't. We want to convince you to be one of the planners.

Perhaps a story of our real-life experiences in financial planning can help here. Among the large number of physicians we have met over the last twenty years, many did not have a financial plan, specifically one that focused on retirement. And when the magic age nears when an individual seeks to reduce the number of hours worked or to actually eliminate them and fully retire (which in today's definition of retirement means beginning to rely on retirement savings-based *cash flow*), the expectations for cash flow to support a comfortable retirement may fall short for lack of adequate sources for desired monthly income. Let's look at one of these physicians; he's an absent-minded general practitioner we'll call Dr. Jones (as in all cases in this book, "Dr. Jones" is a fictional character, compiled from experiences we've had throughout our years of practice). In 1970, when he was thirty-five years old, he set a financial goal for his retirement years using a simple formula. He was going to make sure he retired with $3 million in savings, because long ago he attended a lecture by a financial planner who said it would be good to retire with $1.5 million in the bank. At 5% interest, this would yield $75,000 per year without touching the principal, so theoretically Dr. Jones and his wife would be all set, however long they lived in retirement. They owned two homes, one in Chicago and another on the West Coast of Florida. They would sell the Chicago home, add the proceeds of this sale to the money he had saved, and, just to be safe, Dr. Jones would make sure he doubled the financial planner's advice and put $3 million away for retirement. So, Dr. Jones believed that when he reached the magic age of retirement, he would have $3 million in the bank, and another $750,000 in proceeds from selling his home. That would yield $187,500 in annual income forever, according to his calculations, well above the $170,000 he thought he and his wife would need to spend each year when they retired to Florida.

But it didn't work out that way. In 2010, the year Dr. Jones wanted to retire, he and his wife were in for a rude awakening. As we mentioned in introducing him, Dr. Jones was a conservative man, and he never moved his money out of the savings account in his local bank. He didn't pay attention to the fact that interest rates on his account had fallen to 3%, then 2%, and then even less. This was problem number one; his withdrawals for cash flow would now either have to be reduced to less than half his previous projection, or he would have to risk running out of savings if he took the projected amount of money out of the account each year. Next, he also didn't anticipate some of the expenses his family would incur, and wound up taking out a second mortgage on his Chicago home to fund home improvements and to pay for his children's college educations. Worse, the crash of 2008 reduced the value of his home by another $200,000. So, even though he had planned for capital gains taxes when he sold his house, he was only able to net about $400,000, a little more than half of what he expected to add to his retirement savings, after accepting a lower offer than anticipated on the sale and paying off the second mortgage. And third, he neglected to keep up with the details of his flood insurance on the house in Florida; as the value of that property increased, he never increased the coverage amounts beyond what it was worth forty years earlier, when he bought it. A hurricane struck a few years before he wanted to retire, and he chose to finance needed repairs through a second mortgage on the retirement home, leaving him with about $10,000 in additional annual expenses for the first fifteen years of his retirement. All told, Dr. Jones and his wife went from a plan that seemed comfortable when it was set up thirty years before retirement to one that was in pretty rough shape when he reached retirement age. Annual income of $187,500 became less than $70,000 without touching the principal he had saved, and his expenses went from $170,000 to $180,000 with the second mortgage on his Florida home. What was supposed to be a $17,000 cushion turned out to be a $110,000 deficit each year. And what was supposed to be a comfortable retirement plan turned out to be anything but.

This is an extreme example of a doctor creating a plan early in his career, and then allowing it to proceed on "auto-pilot," without checking on his plan's performance in a changing world. If Dr. Jones had left his financial details to others, he would have been better off; even if he engaged them solely to follow the details of whether his assets were appreciating in a way that was consistent with his vision, he might have been able to avoid the disastrous personal consequences of his failure to plan for disasters of a more natural kind. A more diversified portfolio of assets—one of the most basic ways in which an individual can manage risk over the long term—and regular updates of his flood insurance policy to make sure it kept up with the increasing value of his Florida home, are two simple steps that would have made all the difference. Even with the reduction in cash he was able to realize when selling his Chicago home, Dr. Jones would still be able to withdraw $170,000 per year from his $3.4 million retirement savings, and he wouldn't need the additional $20,000 per year to pay off his Florida home's second mortgage if he had kept his flood insurance up to date. That $170,000 would have matched his projected annual expenses—without a cushion perhaps, but close enough to make adjustments to either lower his annual spending or find a way to increase cash flow from his savings. As it turned out, Dr. Jones decided to work another five years to pay off his Florida mortgage, accumulate additional savings, and move them into a higher-yield mutual fund. Of course, even though it wasn't the least of his problems, he also had to pay taxes on his annual income through these years. He eventually found the retirement "plan" he thought he had in place five years later, when he was seventy years old.

Unfortunately, many other physicians have found themselves in situations similar to Dr. Jones's. They realized too late that their cash flow might run out and assets would be depleted because they didn't fully understand how cash flow and risk management work. Many of them don't fully understand how to plan for income needs during retirement, how much income they can draw every month, and other factors that come into play when a person or a couple retires. In many cases, new retirees find that they may not have enough retirement savings to support the cash flow they need, and therefore they either have to postpone retirement or adjust their lifestyle to live within the limits of lower cash flow income. In addition, negative returns in the market can further devalue retirement assets, and fear kicks in—adding more stress in the person's life, perhaps even causing harm to the retiree's health. Dr. Jones's situation was simple enough to illustrate the basic concept of not just setting up a financial plan but *managing* it, and the need to enlist help from a professional manager if a physician chooses not to get involved in these management responsibilities. The real world doctors face today is far more complex than the example of Dr. Jones; there are many more things that can change or go wrong, and there are also a number of excellent tools and resources that can be used to manage risks and protect both assets and income streams.

At its most basic level, our advice is to have a solid and secure plan, not based on assumptions, but based on guarantees that protect asset levels or future cash flow. This is a vital part of retirement planning. The tools and resources necessary to accomplish this may be available through government agencies, insurance providers, financial institutions, or a number of other programs that offer secure options for protecting savings designed to provide cash flow in retirement. Simply making assumptions that a given "round number" of retirement savings will be adequate is no way to approach the development of a sound financial plan. Dr. Jones isn't the only physician who thought he was saving enough for a comfortable retirement, but instead was disappointed because he relied on these assumptions alone. Assumptions may not always come true.

Like Dr. Jones, many people confuse financial planning with retirement planning, thinking these concepts are one and the same. They are not. Retirement planning is important, but it is only one part of a comprehensive financial plan. Everyone, but especially high-wealth individuals like many physicians, may not understand the concept of risk and may in fact be chasing returns. Education and understanding "behavioral finance" is a very important aspect of prudent financial planning. The concept of "behavioral finance" refers to the way in which we react to certain situations, good or bad. These reactions may be seen as being psychological in nature, but they definitely have effects on an individual's financial plan. One example is selling equity positions when the stock market drops by a certain percentage during a certain period of time. Financial planners like us have seen many cases where clients buy and sell or make a trade in their portfolios at the wrong time, simply because of their emotional reaction to unexpected changes in their holdings. Earlier in the introduction, we promised not to provide a list of "rules" for managing your finances, but this is a case when at least one rule can be highly valuable: when you set up a financial plan to save money for future uses such as retirement, think of the concept of risk in the earliest stages of that plan. Diversify, diversify, diversify. Place some of your funds in "guaranteed" accounts that promise small but reliable gains. And when you put other assets into instruments with higher risk (like the stock market), be prepared for these funds to rise and fall in value. But don't let emotions rule your decisions after setting up these funds. Unless you've picked too many "dogs" in the stocks you've selected for the risky portion of your holdings, ride out the changes and remember that, depending on the precise nature of the "guarantees" offered by your investment company, and that company's overall financial strength, there should be other parts of your plan that remain intact regardless of wild changes in your risky funds. If that doesn't work for you, then maybe it might be best not to invest in risky instruments at all. But make these decisions early and stick with them as much as possible. Emotional investors, like bad poker players, very often lose in the end.

Other emotional behaviors that may have a negative impact on the outcome of your financial plan may include evaluating the performance of your portfolio against the holdings of others, such as family members, friends, or professional colleagues. We have found this to be particularly true for a number of our physician clients; they sometimes listen to recommendations from other physicians, either because they know their colleagues are smart, or because they believe people in the same profession probably share some basic financial circumstances. This is not only a case in which emotions may get the best of individuals trying to stay on course in their financial plans; it's also a situation in which these physicians let assumptions get in the way of sound thinking. Just because one person had a great experience doesn't mean that this same experience would be best for another individual. Your friend or colleague may have different goals that are inconsistent with the plan you've created for yourself and your family. Or this individual may not be financially astute enough to make the right decision about how to protect the gains that have made him or her so happy. For example, this other individual may have decided not to take profits when there's been substantial gain in an investment program. Most people think that these gains will continue, and are disappointed when a correction takes place and losses wipe out these "paper" gains. These are a few introductory examples of the behavioral aspects of a financial plan.

As complex as retirement planning can be, there are other factors to consider in developing a plan—factors that professional financial advisors see all the time. Various types of insurance—medical, disability, life, home/auto/umbrella, and long-term care—can protect assets or provide alternative revenue streams in unforeseen circumstances. Short-term investments to generate revenue, cash emergency funds, long-term investments such as businesses and real estate, and many other investment instruments (mutual funds, annuities, etc.) can add to the success of a physician's plan, or limit that success if they are not properly considered and managed. Another important concept to consider when developing a retirement plan is the difference between the "accumulation" phase of saving for retirement, and the "distribution" phase when savings are actually spent. Even these seemingly simple concepts can include hidden surprises that can derail even the most carefully-planned retirement. Part Three of this book will go into further details about retirement planning concepts, understanding risks, behavioral finance, and other key elements to consider in developing a successful financial plan.

As noted above in the introduction, the decision to run your own practice, either by yourself or in partnership with other medical professionals, brings another round of financial planning requirements. Choosing the right types of insurance, and the correct levels of coverage, is critical for practice owners. So are all the additional responsibilities that come with managing and compensating employees. In addition to all the specific benefits offered to employees—group medical and dental plans, Department of Labor requirements for minimum coverage and disclosures of information about employee benefits, cafeteria plans, and various retirement benefits—there is the most important reason for offering benefits in the first place—to recruit and retain quality employees. Like the personal, non-financial factors that must be considered in developing an individual plan, there are business mission, quality care standards, and other elements of a practice's "core values" that are not in themselves financial, but which have undeniable impacts on a physician's finances and practice management.

For individuals and small business owners, including private practitioners, another critical element of financial planning is cash management. For individuals who earn all their money through salaries, this is a relatively simple matter of translating one's financial plan into a budget in which income exceeds expenses, and the accumulation of savings for long-term purposes and short-term emergencies. Managing debt is a critical element of personal cash planning; while many people think debt is to be avoided at all costs, in reality, most of us purchase major assets like our homes and automobiles through mortgages and car loans, and there are other times when it makes sense to borrow money instead of using one's savings. Debt consolidation, either through home equity loans, refinancing, or the opportunity to take out new loans with more favorable interest rates or payment terms, is another opportunity for anyone to improve cash flow. It's important to remember that insurance coverage, even though it is not "cash management" in the strictest of definitions, can support cash management by reducing the number of emergencies that would otherwise drain emergency funds. Personal insurance strategies are covered in Chapter 9. We will revisit cash management for individuals in Chapter 10.

Small business owners, including physicians owning their own practices, will have more complex cash planning needs. The definitions may be the same as what we recommend for individuals: making sure income exceeds day-to-day expenses, long-term savings, and short-term funds for emergencies, but for a business, "long-term savings" is part of planning for investments in office space, medical equipment, "staffing up" during times of expansion, and other needs for cash a business often brings to its owners. Short-term emergencies can be much larger with a business, and the same insurance option should be explored as a way to lower the risk of paying for these out-of-pocket (i.e. in cash) vs. relying on a well-chosen insurance policy. Debt financing for many business expenses, both capital and operating, is an option that every business owner faces, which gives us the opportunity to introduce the concept of a "hurdle rate" that applies in deciding whether to take on debt and a variety of other cash planning evaluations. Basically, in the case of debt, this is the calculation of how the projected expense of debt repayment compares with projected additional revenue from the debt-funded expansion (new equipment, additional staff, etc.). If projected added revenue exceeds the interest rate for a business loan, conventional wisdom says an owner should take on debt. If calculations are uncertain, or if a loan's interest rate exceeds projected revenue growth, the answer may be no, or at least it requires additional thought. Tax considerations are another big part of business cash management: there are some loans that are more tax-favorable than others, and there are similar options in savings methods. Cash planning is among the most essential reasons for business owners to consult with a qualified financial and tax advisor, since many of these options can be complex and some of the best strategies may not be obvious to individuals who are inexperienced with tax considerations, differences among loans and savings accounts, and other elements of a sound cash plan. We will take a more detailed look at business cash planning in Chapter 7.

To introduce the broad concepts that are included in financial planning, we have included two graphics. Both show the elements of a sound financial plan in order of importance, from the most basic "foundation" components that every financial plan should include to the more specialized tools that can be included in a more complex plan. The first graphic, the "Personal Financial Planning Pyramid," can be found on page 29; it looks at financial plans from the viewpoint a physician might select when looking at ways to build assets and manage risks for the benefit of himself or herself and family members. All physicians, regardless of whether they are salaried employees of a large medical institution or small business owners, will find the concepts in this pyramid to be helpful. The second graphic, the "Business Financial Planning Pyramid," takes a different perspective. It includes the tools and resources a small business owner might use to create and manage a successful plan. Physicians who own and operate private practices, or who are part of a medical group with other physicians and providers, will find these concepts relevant in addition to those introduced in the first pyramid. All of the concepts shown in both of the pyramids will be covered in subsequent chapters of this book.

Physicians Pension & Insurance Services
SRS Business & Personal Insurance Services, Inc.

PERSONAL FINANCIAL PLANNING PYRAMID

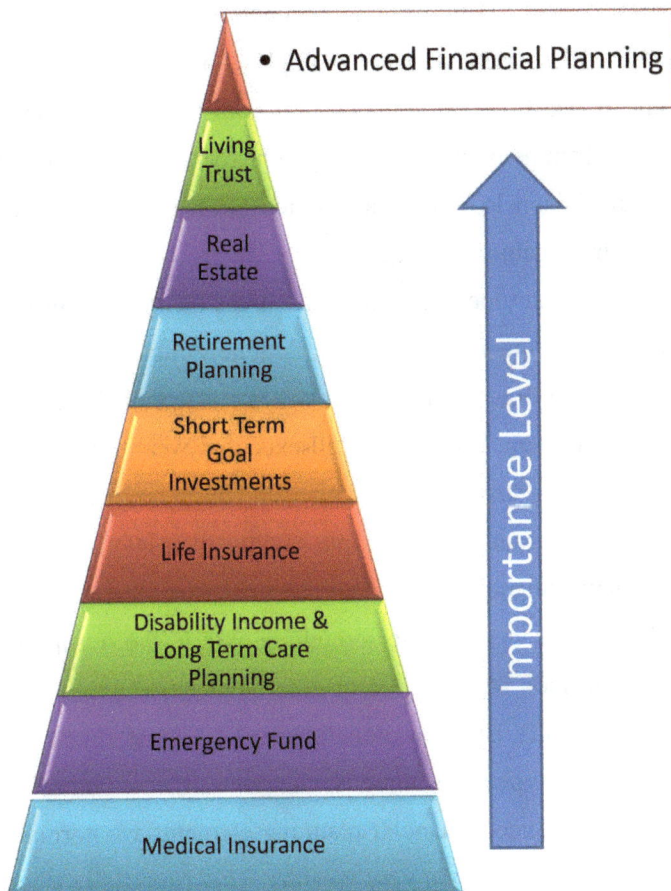

- Advanced Financial Planning

Living Trust

Real Estate

Retirement Planning

Short Term Goal Investments

Life Insurance

Disability Income & Long Term Care Planning

Emergency Fund

Medical Insurance

Importance Level

A GENERAL INTRODUCTION TO THE TWO FINANCIAL PLANNING PYRAMIDS

This first of two financial pyramids introduces the financial tools, resources, and products that are included in any financial plan. There are three different types of these tools, resources, and products, and they are always organized in the same order of priority by professional financial advisors. These are: (1) risk management strategies; (2) wealth accumulation tools; and (3) fine tuning products. The first and most important resources—risk management strategies—are important because they prevent the hard work conducted in wealth management and fine tuning programs from being wasted through unexpected and/or avoidable losses. Financial advisors love risk management strategies. Let me repeat that. We love risk management strategies.

The second type of financial resources includes wealth management tools. These are the programs most of our new clients expect we will spend the bulk of our time discussing when we create their financial plans. And they are important, no doubt. Well-executed wealth management strategies are vital to a strong financial plan, and there are many interesting techniques that can transform a simple savings plan into a high-performance wealth management strategy. But unless risks are anticipated and managed first, these tools can become something akin to the Acropolis in Athens. Beautiful to look at; evidence of great conceptual genius and advanced engineering skills. But ruins nonetheless.

The third type of resource is what we call "fine tuning" in this book. It includes advanced financial planning elements we normally think apply only to those who are very wealthy. This is partially true. Physicians are often included in the category we call "high-wealth individuals," and therefore some of these more advanced products and resources will be relevant to the financial plans readers of this book seek to develop. Living trusts, unique tax treatments, tax-managed investing, and creative estate planning techniques may be excellent ways for those few individuals and families with large income streams and extensive assets to protect their net worth. We will discuss these and other advanced financial planning tools and concepts later, in Part Four. But it is only partially true that some of these techniques are reserved only for the very wealthy. The concepts behind them can be adapted for use in anyone's financial plans, even if they are held back as inactive elements at the beginning, to be implemented later. Fine tuning elements may be in themselves either risk management or wealth accumulation strategies, but they apply in such limited circumstances that they are best included in this third, advanced type of resource for financial planners. Some of these advanced tools and resources are so advanced that they are included in the somewhat redundantly named "advanced financial planning" triangle at the top of the pyramid, but that is the subject of Chapter 12. There is much to learn and discuss before then.

EXPLAINING THE INDIVIDUAL "FINANCIAL PLANNING PYRAMID"

The elements of an individual financial plan shown on page 29 begin with medical insurance. Because one of the key functions of any financial plan is protection against unforeseen risks, this financial tool is listed first. The health of a family's breadwinner—in this case, a physician—is an obvious reason for including medical insurance as the most basic element of an individual financial plan. Medical insurance pays for needed care in the event of illness or injury, with a goal of returning the physician to health and work as soon as possible. But there is an equally obvious reason for including medical insurance as the foundation of an individual financial plan that is a clue to how professional financial advisors think, and how we look out for the best interests of our clients. No one needs to tell a doctor that unforeseen medical expenses can be extraordinarily expensive, and the risk of needing to spend one's own money to pay these bills is the most serious threat to anyone's financial assets. This is a risk that only increases when a physician has a family; other family members may also fall ill or become injured, potentially requiring these same large and unforeseen expenses to be paid. Medical insurance may not be glamorous, but few foundations are. It is without doubt the base on which any individual financial plan must be built.

The second element of a sound individual financial plan is an emergency fund. "Saving for a rainy day" is almost as familiar a phrase for financial planners as "an ounce of prevention is worth a pound of cure" is for people in the field of health care. Making sure there is always access to cash that may be needed without warning is a key part of financial planning; it offers a degree of security any individual or family needs to keep things in focus when emergencies arise. Trying to handle a sudden emergency can be bad enough, but having to do so while at the same time scrambling for money can be devastating.

Other important elements of an individual financial plan include disability income and long-term care planning. Similar to medical insurance, these elements of a financial plan protect a physician and help his or her family control financial risks in the event the policy holder is ill or injured and unable to earn the income the individual and family members require to continue with their lifestyle. Disability income and long-term care planning are actually two separate animals. Disability income planning is typically covered with the purchase of an insurance policy that provides "replacement income" for the physician and his or her family while the policy holder is unable to work. Long-term care planning is also most likely an insurance policy, but it is structured to pay the costs of care provided in a rehabilitation facility, nursing home, or other institution for a policy holder who requires such care. In some cases, these policies may make payments directly to the providers of this care instead of to the policy holder him/herself.

Life insurance, the next step up in our personal financial planning pyramid, is a financial tool most people think they know well. Without giving too much away in the introduction to this book, there are a number of surprising variations in life insurance and how it can be used as part of a financial plan. And its location in the pyramid is also an illustration of how financial advisors think—providing good insights into the conversations we encourage all readers of this book to have with one of these professionals at some point in the near future. First, notice that three of the four most important elements of a personal financial plan are insurance products, or more correctly defined, ways to *manage risks*. And when insurance is defined in this way, all of the first four elements of a sound individual financial plan, including an emergency fund, are ways to manage risks. Individuals who take on the responsibility of developing their own financial plans typically concentrate on retirement planning, and managing investment portfolios in long-term savings accounts. These are, of course, parts of any good financial plan, but they are not the first elements of a plan developed with the help of a professional financial advisor. We concentrate on ways to build wealth that remains as secure as possible, even in the face of unforeseen developments. Risk management is the element we see more clearly than other individuals, and the one we bring to the table whenever we begin our work with clients seeking a strong financial plan.

The other elements at the top of the individual financial planning pyramid—short term goal investments, retirement planning, real estate, and living trusts—are perhaps more familiar, or should we say more expected parts of a financial plan. Whether they are physicians or people engaged in any other sort of business, our clients come to us expecting these tools to be included in their plans. They also understand that we can provide valuable assistance in explaining the complex details of each tool, and to help in selecting the particular type or style of these financial tools that is right for them. Still, we always enjoy the educational role we play in these conversations with our clients. No one thinks about them in the ways we do. For example, most of our clients "get" the fact that retirement planning has two major stages—accumulation and distribution—but they think this is just a basic definition of what retirement planning is. It's not. Each of these two stages requires active management to make sure the plan is performing properly. Retirement plans work best when they're constantly evaluated, updated, and adjusted. Simply putting away an arbitrary sum—even the maximum arbitrary sum into a 401(k) plan—isn't enough anymore. And, except for the risk management foundation of any individual financial plan, there is no other single element in which risk plays such an important role. In fact, the emotional aspects of dealing with risk in one's retirement plan often require their own management strategy.

The intricacies of financial tools at the top of the pyramid are nearly endless, and while they are fascinating to financial advisors and certain high-wealth individuals, they are not the main subject matter for this book. These concepts are introduced and explained in basic detail. But, as the narrowing of the pyramid illustrates, there is much more to be gained by work on the broader first elements of a financial plan.

Next, we'll take a look at our second introductory illustration, the "Business Financial Planning Pyramid," on page 36.

EXPLAINING THE BUSINESS "FINANCIAL PLANNING PYRAMID"

Not surprisingly, the foundation of this second financial pyramid is a basic risk management tool, general liability and property insurance. These types of insurance protect businesses from perhaps the most unpredictable and costly of all threats—lawsuits from individuals and other entities who claim the business is responsible for injury, loss, or damages they seek to recover through litigation. Lawsuits don't directly affect the health of the defendants against whom they're brought, although some might argue otherwise, given the stress these unpredicted and devastatingly costly events may bring to business owners. Still, the analogy between what medical insurance provides for individuals and what general liability and property insurance provide for business owners is a good one. Financial advisors may find it interesting to ponder whether, in terms of sheer dollar cost, unpredicted medical expenses or unpredicted legal expenses are the greater risk to small business owners today. But, given the readers we're trying to reach with this book, we'll stick with our belief that money spent on medical expenses is a better investment in the health of our society.

It may be a bit surprising to some readers that the next level in our business financial planning pyramid is workers' compensation insurance. This is something many employees see as a minor component of their benefits package, one that is structured in such a way that its benefits aren't paid until a long waiting period is completed, and even when they're paid, are too small to realistically cover lost income when a worker becomes disabled due to a work-related injury. In fact, that's the point. Physicians who are either salaried employees or owners of a small business need to realize the inadequacy of most employer-provided disability insurance programs, and should take steps to find coverage for themselves that can

Physicians Pension & Insurance Services
SRS Business & Personal Insurance Services, Inc.
360° FINANCIAL

BUSINESS FINANCIAL PLANNING PYRAMID

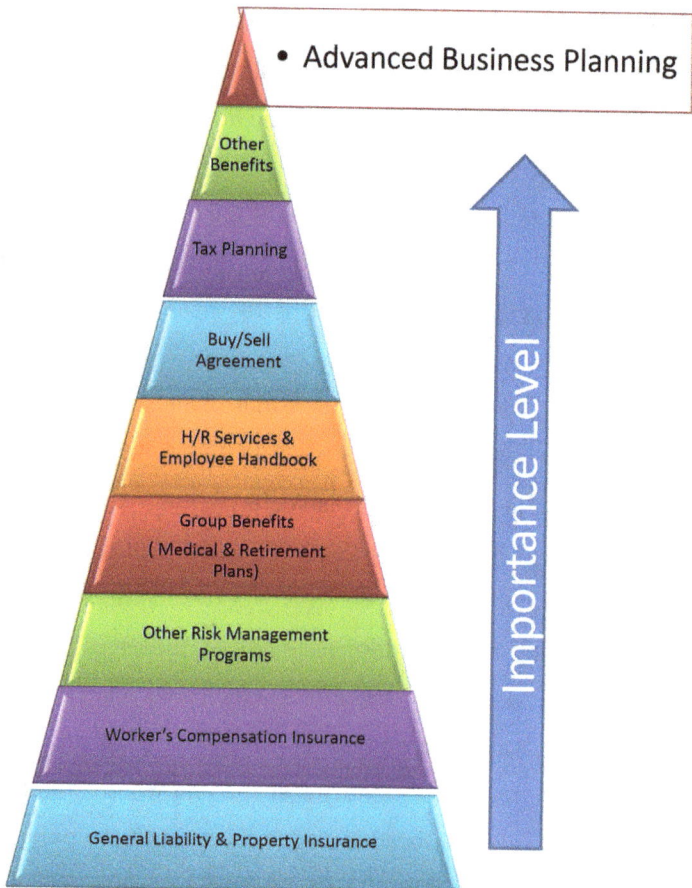

- Advanced Business Planning

Other Benefits

Tax Planning

Buy/Sell Agreement

H/R Services & Employee Handbook

Group Benefits (Medical & Retirement Plans)

Other Risk Management Programs

Worker's Compensation Insurance

General Liability & Property Insurance

Importance Level

provide the income they and their families would need in the event of a long absence from work. Individual disability insurance policies are expensive, and have their own long lists of potential exclusionary clauses that may stand in the way of even the most careful individual's efforts to buy adequate disability insurance. Physicians typically earn high incomes, and individual disability plans that pay these levels of benefits are difficult—but not impossible—to find (or to assemble, in some cases). More complicated is the question of how a small business owner can structure his or her own disability insurance coverage; in some states, care must be taken to make sure a business offers the same benefit package to all employees and to the owners as well; in these states, owners may need to make separate arrangements for additional risk protection through personal plans, or through other types of insurance such as "business continuity" coverage. Still, disability insurance (and related products) are extremely important for physicians who are small business owners. Should they become disabled, they'll need income to not only provide for their families, but to also cover the operations and overhead expenses of their medical practice. Again, there are ways for physicians to provide this important coverage for themselves, but they require some creativity and what might be called choreography, if there is such a thing in financial planning.

Group benefits (medical and retirement plans) are the next step in the business financial planning pyramid; these are optional programs a small business owner can build into the company's employee benefits package to benefit everyone, including the owner. The retirement plans included in this step are solid wealth accumulation tools, and there are many more of them than the range of 401(k) plans that are familiar to many of us. The medical plans listed in this step of the pyramid are an example of additional employee benefits small business owners can offer their employees and themselves to manage risks as well as accumulate wealth. These group plans rarely offer coverage that is as comprehensive or reliable as individual policies, but they can bring a level of protection to which additional programs can be added. And, because there really is such a thing as choreography in business owner financial planning, it may be important to implement group and individual plans in an order that allows business owners to achieve their risk management or wealth accumulation goals.

The human resource services and employee handbook at the next step in the business pyramid bring us back to the risk management strategies we love. Well-trained employees can help reduce risks in the daily operation of any business; human error is at the heart of many professional liability claims, personal injuries in the workplace, or even labor law violations. In a physician's office, these risks are even larger. Patient confidentiality, medical malpractice, discrimination, and other potential liabilities require additional attention to employee training, documented policies and procedures, and other human resource strategies.

The remaining steps at the top of the business pyramid—buy/sell agreements, tax planning, and other benefits—are "fine tuning" resources. A buy/sell agreement is probably required when a small business includes multiple owners, whether that business is a partnership or a corporation. In the event of death, disability, retirement, or departure of one of the owners, this type of agreement can allow the remaining owners to continue operations, while the departing owner or his/her heirs receive payment for the share of the business owned by that individual. Tax planning brings a sort of academic question: is it risk management, or wealth accumulation? Either way, a good tax attorney, qualified CPA, and experienced financial advisor can work together to provide extremely valuable assistance when a practice grows large, or when practices merge to form larger entities. The new world of health care management brought about by the Affordable Care Act of 2010 (ACA, also known as "health reform" or "Obamacare") may bring more of these types of mergers as multiple health care institutions join forces to become the new "Affordable Care Organizations" (ACOs) designed to provide comprehensive care to large groups of American citizens, receiving capitated global payments that replace traditional "fee for service" payment systems.

◄ ● ►

Other than running out of money in retirement, missing mortgage payments on the family home, or running out of cash during the operation of your practice, there are few elements of a financial plan that are universally right or wrong (in this case, all three of these are objectively wrong). But without a well-developed plan that is constructed with a physician's individual situation in mind—or even worse, without a plan at all—there is certainly the potential for an objectively wrong answer for many of the financial questions every doctor must face. The good news, though, is that a well-constructed plan includes a broad range of possibilities for the right answer to these same questions. If someone's idea of discretionary spending is going out to dinner with the family once every week, the money required to do that can be quantified and factored into a viable plan.

On the other hand, for someone whose idea of discretionary spending is a summer home in Florida with a yacht, a different right answer means putting a larger amount of money aside to finance the home and buy the yacht, as long as these expenses fit within that person's overall budget for income and expenses. So can the choice of being an employee or an entrepreneurial owner of a private practice. Even the non-financial goal of serving as a tenured professor of medicine at a prestigious medical school can be part of a successful financial plan for a physician. In this case, there are predictable expenses involved in the advanced educational degrees required for becoming a professor, and the additional (or perhaps lower) income associated with this status as compared to "simply" practicing medicine.

In summary, before going into detail about any elements of a physician's individual, small business, or career-specific financial plan, we can say that the importance of planning, and of starting a plan with an honest self-assessment of financial and non-financial goals, cannot be overstated. Any plan that does not begin with this important first step is just a distraction.

PART TWO
PRACTICE AND FINANCIAL MANAGEMENT
FOR PHYSICIANS

CHAPTER 3

RISK MANAGEMENT IN A CHANGING WORLD– INSURANCE, PATIENT PRIVACY, AND ELECTRONIC MEDICAL RECORDS

INTRODUCTION TO PRACTICE MANAGEMENT FOR PHYSICIANS

Physicians and their staff must be passionate about their work. After all, doctors are privileged to work in one of the most important professions in the world. It's a profession that many people believe is not just about money, but is about helping people and making a difference in their lives. In many cases, not to be overly dramatic, medical care is nothing short of a life-saving business. By the very practice of the career they have chosen, physicians communicate their unique commitment to this rewarding field. In this context, it is important to offer some initial thoughts about the importance of financial planning advice for physicians before plunging into the details. We've all been at conferences about the management of health care, and some of us have participated in panel discussions about the importance of "Mission *and* Margin." Even though the second half of this phrase is what professional financial managers stress almost as much as risk management itself, we want to be sure to keep our conversation about the business side of medical practice in perspective. All clients seeking our advice have non-financial goals that must be taken into account when creating a financial plan. Everyone wants to enjoy life, and the definition of how each of us will pursue happiness (to borrow a phrase) is a highly personal matter. Financial consequences flow from these choices, to be sure, but a good financial advisor will begin by talking about these non-financial life goals before diving into the tools that can make such goals easier to achieve.

With physicians, the career goal of providing medical care to people so they can live longer and healthier lives brings non-financial goals into the workplace. Other lines of work do this as well, but few combine the commitment to do good with the financial opportunities to do well that doctors may find in their careers. Throughout this book, we will discuss details behind risk management strategies using language such as "protection against loss" or "in the event of disability" or other similar phrases. If these discussions seem to overlook the human side of life events such as illness, injury, or death, we apologize. Medical providers see the human side of these "losses" and "risks" in a way few others do, and do so on a daily basis. We understand that these considerations often outweigh any financial interpretation of these words, and want to be sure our advice is never taken to mean that we are unaware of these choices. However, in our years of providing financial advice, we have seen some physicians who become so immersed in their work that they ignore financial concerns. This attitude doesn't mean these concerns go away; they remain relevant, and require management. Whether a physician chooses to manage his or her own finances, or prefers leaving these matters to others, it is always wise to discuss this choice with a trusted financial advisor. As financial advisors, we're used to engaging in conversations with all our clients. When we do things like write this book, we leave the world of dialogue for one in which we've set our controls to "output only." But this introduction to risk management, wealth accumulation, and the details of strategies and techniques to include in a physician's financial plan are secondary to whatever life goals that plan is designed to support.

We'll begin with risk management, one of our favorite topics. In addition to the previous chapter's advice about managing the operations of a physician's practice, there are several risk-management strategies that can be considered as both day-to-day administration and financial management. Business insurance is a topic covered later in Part Three of this book, but there are several other insurance products that are essential to the management of a successful doctor's office, or even the career management of a physician who is a salaried employee of a hospital or other large medical institution. In addition to these insurance products, doctors must also manage the risks that have come to the profession with the use of electronic medical records and corresponding requirements that doctors keep this information confidential. Some doctors may see this as a vise that has them caught between two irresistible forces: as they are encouraged to use electronic medical records in order to improve patient care by coordinating the services of different providers, they are being asked to protect these records from hackers that doctors cannot detect, let alone fight. The answer—insurance—may not be the best answer, but for now it remains the best way to protect a practice from lawsuits that could result from a data breach.

Following is a partial list of risk-management strategies doctors must consider in the management of a modern medical practice.

MALPRACTICE INSURANCE

The most obvious insurance coverage for physicians is malpractice insurance. It may need to take different forms depending on where a physician practices, and whether he or she is an employee of a health care organization or owner/partner at a private practice group, but there can be no doubt that malpractice insurance is essential for any practicing medical professional.

Note our use of the term "practicing medical professional" here. It's intentional. In today's world, malpractice insurance for a physician alone is often not enough coverage. Modern physicians' offices include other professionals—nurses, nurse practitioners, and physician assistants, for example—and these individuals are subject to the same risks as doctors themselves. Also at risk is the practice where they work. Doctors who have not updated their coverage may be surprised to learn that their coverage might not extend to everyone who needs it. We recommend that doctors stay diligent and vigilant to make sure their malpractice coverage matches the way their practices are structured. Any added premiums to accomplish this are well worth the cost.

Other ways to manage the risk of litigation in this area involve the application of "clinical practice guidelines" (CPGs). The American College of Physicians (ACP) has been producing these guidelines since 1981, and they are frequently updated as the practice of medicine (and related state laws and regulations) change. References to CPGs are sometimes made in litigation by both plaintiffs and defendant medical professionals, and their impact on individual lawsuits cannot always be predicted. However, it is worth noting that these guidelines exist, and that they have been used in several states to try and reform their legal systems as they apply to malpractice claims and lawsuits. Learning about their potential influence on malpractice risk management is another recommendation. The ACP website, (https://www.acponline.org/clinical_information/guidelines/guidelines/cgc.htm) is a good place to begin research on this topic. So is the American Medical Association's Journal of Ethics, (http://journalofethics.ama-assn.org/2011/01/hlaw1-1101.html). Efforts to reduce the cost and risks associated with malpractice litigation, also called "tort reform," are being considered and debated by several states; they are also the subject of national studies by a number of medical and legal advocacy groups. Solutions such as caps on malpractice awards, assumption of risk by enterprises as opposed to individual physicians, and replacement of the current adversarial jury trial method for adjudicating cases with a "less formal process" are a few of the ideas for reforming the United States' system of resolving malpractice claims.[1] It should be noted that in all cases, when a court awards a claim and its value exceeds the limits of all insurance coverage, the individual physician him/herself will be personally liable for this additional amount.

HIPAA PATIENT CONFIDENTIALITY AND CYBER ATTACK RISKS

Other insurance required by physicians, regardless of where they are employed, include protection from risks associated with accidental disclosure of confidential patient information, or the malicious distribution of this information by criminal outsiders "hacking" into today's electronic medical records (EMRs). This relatively new type of risk is increasing rapidly and must be addressed by every physician. The medical industry is one of the largest targets for hacking attacks, and most doctors are not

---

1 http://www.ncbi.nlm.nih.gov/pmc/articles/PMC2628513/

prepared in several ways. First, they may not have the resources to prevent sophisticated hackers from accessing their EMRs. Second, they may
not fully understand the risk of personal and financial liability they face
from these attacks. Third, they may engage in online behavior that unnecessarily exposes them to cyber attacks, such as not using secure e-mail
communication, or always sending encrypted files when communicating
about their patients, along with other counter-measures. Finally, they may
not have purchased adequate insurance coverage to protect their assets and
income in the event of a criminal cyber attack.

How can physicians protect themselves and their practices from this
new and growing risk? The answers are in education and training—for
themselves and for their business office staff, along with other medical
professionals with whom they collaborate in providing care. Further, they
need to understand the laws and how they apply in cases of criminal cyber attacks, in order to ensure that all possible countermeasures are taken
in advance of any potential compromise of their confidential data. This
includes avoidance of mistakes and inadvertent violations of HIPAA-de-
fined patient confidentiality within a practice or health care institution,
measures to prevent unlawful cyber attacks on EMRs, and insurance protection in the event these practical counter-measures are insufficient. Current federal law governing protection of patient confidentiality is called the
"Health Information Technology for Economic and Clinical Health Act"
(HITECH). Passed in 2009, this law mandates penalties for medical professionals whose practices violate patient confidentiality based on whether
these violations are committed by an individual who "did not know" (and
by exercising reasonable diligence would not have known), or if violations
were "due to reasonable cause and not to willful neglect," or if violations
were due to willful neglect, or if violations were not corrected after being

discovered. These penalties can be severe; they range from $25,000 to a maximum of $1.5 million per year. Because it is unclear how the terms "reasonable cause" or "willful neglect" are defined, obtaining coverage to protect financial risks from cyber attacks is a new and critical element in every physician's professional liability coverage. [2]

Additional Links:
http://www.dhs.gov/how-do-i/protect-myself-cyber-attacks
And:
http://www.ama-assn.org

OTHER IMPORTANT INSURANCE NEEDS FOR PHYSICIANS

Physicians who own their own practices must evaluate a number of other insurance options to see if they might be beneficial in reducing risk and/or complying with changing government regulations. These include:

Employment Practices Liability (EPL I)

This is an important and often-overlooked form of insurance coverage physicians with employees need to consider. Covered below in Chapter 6, EPL I protects practice owners from damages claimed by current or former employees who believe they were unfairly treated during their employment in the practice, or who believe they were terminated unfairly, or who claim they were the victims of sexual harassment or discrimination.

---

2 http://www.hhs.gov/ocr/privacy/hipaa/administrative/enforcementrule/hitechenforcementifr.html

EPL I coverage helps reduce time-consuming court proceedings, the costs of such litigation, and potential large awards to employees who win these cases. Additional information about EPL I insurance is provided later in Part Three of this book, when we discuss risk management strategies for small business owners. The important protection EPL I insurance provides is that its coverage not only helps protect a physician's assets in the event of litigation, but it also covers the cost of legal and attorney fees and any potential damages that may be awarded. This helps the physician by reducing the risk of having to pay out-of-pocket funds to defend himself or herself. Other insurance policies may not cover these very significant potential financial risks.

Property and Equipment Insurance

Medical practice often involves the use of highly sophisticated and therefore expensive equipment. Protecting these from loss in the event of an accident, fire, theft, or other eventuality is an important risk management responsibility for physicians. The costs of equipment used to diagnose and treat health issues in a physician's office is substantial, and so is the likelihood that new or updated equipment means these machines will need to be replaced on a frequent basis. Practice expansion is also a factor here; adding another provider may be accomplished by "doubling up" on the use of certain technologies, but new staff will eventually mean adding another doctor's office, with its own set of medical devices. Because professional financial advisors always look for ways to manage risks in creating a sound financial plan, the amount of money invested in a doctor's medical equipment is a prime candidate for careful attention. Updating the value of equipment coverage on all insurances is vital.

It may be practical to cover medical equipment through certain Business Owner Policies (BOPs), but expensive and unique medical equipment may be excluded from these policies. Physicians or their business management staff must make sure all of a practice's property, equipment, and even furniture are covered, and frequent reviews of the policies in place for these purposes are part of the overall risk management strategy we recommend.

Self-Insurance

Even with the most careful advance planning, there are many risks that may elude insurance planning through the purchase of commercially-available policies. Insurance companies base their business on actuarial calculations, and these calculations rely on estimating both the likelihood and cost of insurable losses. In some cases, when the likelihood of a loss cannot be predicted, or when the cost of a loss is uncertain (or, in some cases too large for a carrier to consider), insurance companies may not write a policy for the coverage a business owner seeks, or the premiums they demand are unreasonably high and cannot be included in a small business's financial plans. In these cases, businesses may have few alternatives other than setting aside their own funds to be used in the event of such losses. Self-insurance can be a consideration when facing the types of risks that most business owners/physicians have not insured against, which may include reputation risk, terrorism, earthquake, flood, etc.

It's not an easy program to implement, and even when it is the best alternative, self-insurance is rarely the complete answer to a physician's risk management strategy. The same risks that prevent insurance companies from selling policies in these cases remain. A catastrophic loss for a doctor, such as a malpractice lawsuit or total loss of all medical equipment from a fire or flood, will still be the same prohibitively expensive disaster. It's unrealistic for a single small practice to put away enough cash to cover these losses. So what should a physician do in these cases? As we will see in a number of other risk management strategies described throughout this book, the answer lies in putting together a number of partial answers to provide a solution that is the best possible solution for the total risk involved. Self-insurance is rarely the single answer to managing risks commercial policies will not cover, even in the largest of corporations and government agencies. Pooling risks, which is what insurance companies do, is something that is done in many industries, and medical practice is no exception. "Risk pools" are a technique used by a number of similar businesses; they pool funds contributed by many independent organizations into a single fund designed to cover potential losses, and spread the risk among all the businesses participating in the pool. In concept, it looks a lot like what commercial insurance companies do, and that's a good way to look at the idea of self-insurance in general. These pools aren't a complete answer to the "how can anyone pay such an expensive claim?" question, but they do offer the advantage of allowing more of the funds in the risk pool to become available in the event of a loss. Expenses that take away from commercial insurers' cash reserves—such as their large sales forces, or the need for profits to distribute to shareholders—are eliminated by these pools, which at least makes them incrementally more attractive than commercial insurance in some cases.

Self-insurance options include participating in risk pools with other physicians and their practices, or, in some cases, structuring "captive" insurance companies when activities like actuarial calculations of the likelihood and cost of potential losses are necessary to determine the size of a fund that needs to be created to offer adequate coverage for the company or companies involved in a risk pool. These captive insurance companies, which look even more like commercial insurers, are discussed below in Chapter 12, along with other options available to physicians seeking to manage risks your insurance broker can't cover. Remember, however, that self-insurance is only part of the answer; managing unpredictable or potentially catastrophic risks means buying as much commercial insurance as a physician can, and reviewing this insurance to make sure it will still provide the protection for which it was purchased as definitions of losses, limits on the amount of claims paid, and premium levels change over time.

An objective and experienced insurance advisor can also provide insight into future performance of commercial insurance policies in these cases, such as what happens to an insured company after that company files a claim. It's not exactly true or fair to insurance companies, but "conventional wisdom" says that they make money by saying no. Technically, insurers make money by estimating the total cost of claims they will pay in a given year, and then setting premiums for all their customers to a level so that the total revenue from all premiums paid will exceed the total cost of all claimed losses the company pays—plus gains or losses on their investments, operating costs, and other considerations, of course. But at the heart of the insurance business are many professional staff doing nothing else all day except managing risks. For insurance companies, this can mean finding gray areas in their definitions of insurable losses and interpreting them in the insurance company's favor. Engaging the expertise of risk managers who will include all risks—including the risk that an insurance company might not pay the claim a business owner wants to cover—is one of the biggest reasons for seeking help from professional financial advisors and the professional specialists they can bring to the table in a number of situations. "Extreme" insurance is one such area, as are tax planning, real estate, and the evaluation of advanced wealth accumulation tools. There may not be a "best" answer, particularly when choosing between unreasonably expensive insurance coverage and relying on self-insurance alone. But professional insurance specialists will almost certainly be able to provide a better answer.[3]

---

3 http://www.naic.org/cipr_topics/topic_captives.htm.

Chapter 4

DESIGNING A CARING ENVIRONMENT— "BEDSIDE MANNER" FOR TODAY'S MEDICAL PROFESSIONALS, AND MARKETING THE PRACTICE

THERE ARE A NUMBER OF financial planning considerations that are unique to physicians and the practice of medicine; these include the consequences of ways a practice is organized. Whether a physician is a small business owner or an employee of a large hospital dealing with the changes the Affordable Care Act will bring, there are a number of good business practices that can enhance the way a physician delivers care, and succeed in not only meeting the needs of his or her existing patients, but increase the likelihood that other potential patients will seek their care from the physician as well.

We'll start with another kind of physician-specific advice: how to manage a medical practice from an operational standpoint. Making sure quality care is provided in an environment that is conducive to maintaining the unique bond between a doctor and his or her patients is very much a part of any business plan for a practicing physician. Making sure the concepts introduced in this chapter are in place will provide a strong foundation for earning and managing the financial assets that come from a successful medical practice. Here are a few of the things we believe are important to consider in the day-to-day managing of a practice, business office and, above all, the relationship between a doctor and his or her patients.

"KINESTHETICS" AND BODY LANGUAGE; THE "BEDSIDE MANNER" OF THE TWENTY-FIRST CENTURY

Bedside manner is something patients have always used to evaluate the care provided by their doctors. Some physicians may argue that this isn't as important as the practice of sound, science-based medicine, but unless you're a surgeon and your patients are always unconscious, this is no longer the case. There are many tools and educational programs available to help people understand how important body language is in any kind of business environment. For physicians, it is vital to consider how nonverbal communications affect the way they communicate when they're discussing serious and potentially difficult topics with their patients. Looking patients in the eye may seem like a good thing to do in all cases, and in most cases, it probably is. In some cases, it is in fact vital. Delivering bad news, complicated information, or important advice about what a patient can do to manage his or her health in everyday life, certainly requires this kind of nonverbal communication. But in other cases, particularly in today's world of medical practice, using the display of a computer screen, or opening a book or brochure to a relevant page, can be an effective way of communicating information. So can looking away for a moment when thinking about an idea or considering the best answer to a patient's question. Remembering that patients are likely to be nervous or worried about their health requires doctors to be as reassuring as possible, and sometimes too much eye contact with their physician can add to this stress. There is no rule about the optimal percentage of the time a doctor should make eye contact with a patient during a visit; this is a matter of personal choice, and the comfort of the physician is also an important consideration. Like many of the other concepts introduced in this book, we are offering an idea for consideration without making a specific recommendation. Simply thinking about matters like this, however, is a strategy that can lead physicians to be more effective in communicating with their patients, and ultimately more successful in their work.

Another bedside manner/body language is the extent to which a doctor uses gestures in communication with patients. Moving one's hands and arms is a common habit for many people, and can be an unconscious "second nature" type of behavior. But for some people, certain gestures can carry meanings that make them uncomfortable, or feel threatened. Making sure all gestures are "reassuring" and not sudden or aggressive in any way is something to be considered in all interactions between physicians and their patients.

How a physician positions him or herself next to a patient when they are discussing these topics is also worth careful thought. Just like in any business, most doctors have had some training in interpersonal communication, even if this training was as long ago as a high school presentation by a guidance counselor or a presentation from a college career services advisor. Perhaps they have learned the proper way to shake someone's hand, how to sit around a conference table during a meeting, or how a person is dressed; basic information like this is often included in these sorts of programs. Such basic information also applies in many ways to the behavior a doctor exhibits when communicating with, or even when treating his or her patients. Some physicians may think these concepts are extraneous or even irrelevant to the practice of medicine. Knowledge and expertise are what save lives, these doctors say, and the delivery of this expertise is more important than the way it is delivered. But the words of one of my favorite doctors are worth mentioning here. "Everything a doctor does with a patient is care. Talking is care. Listening is care. And the better we talk and listen, the better we are at delivering care."

Here are a few additional thoughts about the importance of good communication with patients. For example, talking down to someone instead of talking in plain language shows respect. Patients may not always stop a physician when hearing the Latin name of a disease or condition, and in cases like this, the opportunity to convey real information is lost. Using English terminology may seem too basic, and if it is, then how about this recommendation: every once in a while, ask a patient if he or she understands the information you're discussing. This simple practice can go a long way to making sure the patient will be able to follow the physician's advice on how to manage his or her health once the office visit is over and the patient either goes to the pharmacy or heads home.

There are also a few more nuanced concepts on "bedside manner," body language, and sensitive communication techniques with patients. One is where a doctor should position him/herself when talking with a patient. I have always believed that if a message is very serious, then *not* sitting directly in front of the patient is probably a better idea. As we discussed earlier in this chapter, when you're sitting face-to-face and are looking a patient straight in the eye while giving a very serious or negative message, the patient may feel even more uncomfortable at a time when it is important to be as sensitive and reassuring as possible. Sitting next to the person, almost as if the doctor and patient are friends, may make the same negative message easier to absorb, understand and comprehend. By paying attention to body language and nonverbal clues in communication, physicians can make their patients feel more comfortable and more relaxed. Efforts to pay attention to patients' feelings are their own form of nonverbal communication; patients can sense these efforts, and appreciate them. There are also very simple practical efforts doctors can make to show concern for their patients; spending an adequate amount of time during exams, and in discussing the patient's health, also show how much doctors care. Patients who believe their doctors care about them are far more likely to engage in open communication. It may be possible that such open communication will lead to a patient bringing new information to the physician during a visit, and this information may give the physician new insights into the care that may be best for his or her patient. When doctors communicate effectively in their work, patients aren't the only individuals who learn during these conversations.

If a physician is intrigued by the idea of how body language can affect communication with patients or even the delivery of care, it may be worth engaging a professional in this field to discuss this idea in more detail. If nothing else, observation by an objective professional can yield insights into things a medical provider does that may support or detract from the effectiveness of their clinical services.

PSYCHOLOGICAL FACTORS TO CONSIDER WHEN DESIGNING A PHYSICIAN'S OFFICE

In any service business, we always think about things that can be done that negatively or positively affect the people around us. For physicians, we'll start with considerations such as how the office's physical space is designed, what colors are used in its décor, and how the office environment makes people feel when they arrive at the office. Making the office feel comfortable and homey is essential in making patients overcome anxiety and relax when they come to the doctor's office. Even background music may also be helpful in relieving some of the stress people have when they arrive. I have seen a number of doctors install aquariums in their waiting areas, which are surprisingly helpful in getting people to calm down and relax. If nothing else, these miniature worlds can be more engaging and alive than the magazines many doctors use to entertain their patients while they wait for their appointments. Which is another message—unintended or not—to consider when designing the waiting room. Magazine articles take time to read; the impression many patients may have is that they are going to spend a lot of time waiting, if they have a choice of multiple magazines to occupy their time. That may or may not be a conclusion doctors want their patients to reach. And the opposite may be true. Since many practices are becoming better at managing their operations and time in waiting rooms is decreasing, patients may no longer have as much time to read as they had in the past.

Thinking about these details is one of the many psychological factors to consider in designing an office. A waiting area isn't just a place to hold patients like inventory on a shelf before they see a doctor. It's a part of the overall "customer experience," to use a potentially annoying phrase. But whether business-related subjects like office décor or considerations of a patient visit as a total experience are comfortable for physicians or not, the truth is that these are important considerations in designing and managing a successful medical practice. Doctors who realize this and do something to stay competitive with other physicians and medical practices in their area may be more successful than those who concentrate on clinical training and medical equipment alone. Staff training and attention to the patient's overall experience may never be included in the definition of health care itself, but the environment in which care is delivered is still an important way in which patients remember the care they receive, and their willingness to return for a next visit or recommend a physician to friends and family members.

One final note about the waiting area is the importance of having nice furniture there, and why. A comfortable and well-maintained waiting area makes people feel worthy and respected when they come to the doctor's office; old, ripped or out of date couches and chairs, or furniture that seems out of place or uncomfortable can be taken as evidence that the doctor does not really care that much about his or her patients. This is an increasingly important consideration in today's competitive health care industry; like it or not, patients have more choice than ever about whom they choose as a medical provider, and they do make judgments based on the experience they have when they enter the business.

Not only should the patient waiting area be designed nicely; so should the examination rooms. They, too, need to be colorful and patient-friendly, with other design elements such as soothing music to release patients' tension. Remember that patients spend time there by themselves in between being escorted by staff and the moment the doctor arrives. As any of us who have been to a hospital recently can observe, many of them, particularly the larger ones, are spending millions of dollars to upgrade and renovate their lobbies, waiting areas, patient rooms, and even nursing stations to make them look nicer and feel more welcoming, so that they attract more people and make patients and visitors want to choose this hospital for future services, or even stay there when that may be required.

Sometimes there can be no end to the creativity employed by the designers of doctors' offices, hospitals, and other health care institutions. Lighting, and particularly soothing music are essential things every doctor's office ought to have. Even a waterfall feature can be an attractive element in the waiting room of a physician's office. Remember that the assurance of quality care and confidentiality are basics that patients—as consumers—expect. The extra touches we're suggesting here are important because the more a patient feels respected and is relaxed and comfortable, the more likely he or she will be able to communicate with the physician about the sensitive subject of their health and their concerns about that health.

LEADERSHIP AND MANAGEMENT

Physicians should know that it is really important for them to step up and become true leaders in their practices. This includes paying attention to the entire practice through strong professional relationships with employees, clear communication about the concerns of their employees as they deal with the inevitable stress of dealing with patients who are more likely to be stressed and possibly difficult to handle, and to make sure sound management systems and structures are in place to delegate and support managerial responsibility throughout the practice's entire staff team. The physician should educate office staff and inspire them to provide the best services each of them can provide. This means that the staff needs to understand the direction that the owner/physician envisions for the practice; the physician should have clear-cut directions for everyone to follow, both in a big-picture sense of the practice's overall mission, and in the day-to-day operation of the office as it serves the patients who rely on the practice for their care.

Unfortunately, we all know physicians who are not in sync with their employees, do not provide clear-cut direction, and expect their staff to understand on their own what they need to be doing. Physicians can no longer try to stay above all of the details of how their office is managed; they need to pay attention to details of their practice as a functioning business. This includes establishing and maintaining mutual respect between the physician and his or her employees, and also making sure that there are competitive compensation packages, for these employees, including benefits and a supportive work environment to attract and retain highly competent employees. After all, the physician can't be everywhere, and cannot expect patients to put up with substandard service from office staff until they actually spend time with the doctor. A practice's employees must be capable of executing the vision of the physician/owner, and must be able to make sure that patients get the treatment they deserve and require.

In this day and age, physicians have—maybe not quite, but almost—become commodities; this is unfortunate but true. If people don't like the way the doctor does business, or the way the doctor's staff treats them, or even how the office looks, then they will find another physician they can trust to deliver their care. Most people no longer have the patience to put up with things that don't make them feel comfortable; and the medical industry is now starting to feel that pressure from consumers, just like any other business. Add all of the changes coming via the health care reform to the changes that are already here, and the sum of these changes makes it more difficult for physicians to succeed in providing health care while they are also thinking about how to manage their practice.

It is imperative that the owner/physician knows how to delegate and get other people to help manage the practice—so that the doctor is not overwhelmed and overworked. For example, many physicians follow the "old school" vision of a private doctor's office and choose to do everything on their own, without hiring qualified or adequate staff to share the enormously complex challenge of providing health care in today's professional environment. In our work with some physicians, we've seen a few who process payroll, manage daily scheduling for staff, supervise employees at the front desk and in the lab, work as their own HR manager, and, in some cases, even do their own billing for insurance claims. When we're asked, or in many cases even when we're not, we tell these doctors that their management practices are a recipe for disaster: exhaustion inevitably sets in, followed by being unprepared for changing business requirements and finally the slide of their practices into the ranks of unsuccessful business-es. Physicians need to inspire their staff to understand that they're in the important business of health care together, and then these same physicians have to learn to delegate. In the old days, physicians could survive without paying attention to business details; it would fall to someone else on staff to pick up on these details in order to "save" the doctor from these distractions and allow him or her to concentrate on the provision of care alone.

That's no longer possible in today's competitive world. Physicians have to worry about the business elements of their practices, including finance, human resources, quality of care, and compliance with ever-more-complicated regulations. They even need to develop and execute a successful marketing program (more on this below). The good news is that if the physician focuses on wider issues in structuring the practice as a business, hires the right people, creates a team, and leads by example in maintaining a practice-wide focus on helping people, revenue will be there and the practice will be successful. Finally, we're often surprised by doctors' reluctance to invest in new equipment when it comes to the business side of a practice. We often see a strange dichotomy between shiny new medical equipment and old, broken-down fax machines, printers, and other office equipment. This not only gives the wrong impression to patients who inevitably see these office machines in use; it also interferes with the efficiency of the practice's staff in completing their tasks, and ultimately it eats away at employee morale. It is important for physicians to remember their responsibility to be great leaders in addition to being great clinicians. Leadership includes understanding the value of an investment of a few hundred dollars in quality machinery and equipment. This not only makes the practice more efficient; it helps establish an environment in which the psychological and emotional factors that are always present among patients visiting their doctors are as well-managed. The confidence these patients feel in an office that is clean, modern, comfortable, and well-managed helps give them confidence in the care they will receive there.

MARKETING AND STAFF TRAINING: STAYING AHEAD OF TODAY'S ONLINE REVIEWS

Decades ago, doctors considered it unethical to advertise their services. That is no longer the case today, but although many physicians place advertisements in publications, on billboards, and use other marketing strategies, most doctors have still not developed a sound marketing approach for today's world of internet-based reviews like Yelp! and other websites. Doctors need to know how to obtain positive public reviews, because most people are now looking at these websites to determine whether or not they're going to go to a specific doctor. We all know that one bad review can ruin a business, or at least lead to the loss of many potential patients or clients. The good news here is that, in many ways, these internet review sites function in exactly the same way as "word of mouth" did, and still does. Physicians' current patients are their number one source of referrals, and how they treat these patients is the best way to ensure positive reviews. This means providing excellent customer service from the time an appointment is made through the time a patient spends in the office, and even how the doctor provides follow-up care and communication. I believe that the physician who goes above and beyond what patients expect will end up not only keeping the vast majority of these patients, but will also receive the positive online reviews that help bring new patients to the office. I even think it would be a great idea for a physician's office to create guidelines and procedures for interacting with patients, and to train staff to go above and beyond in making each patient's experience as welcoming and respectful as possible.

Physicians should also make sure that their patients have the following services available to make communication and access to care as convenient as possible. Below is a story told to us by one of our physician clients about an incident involving one of his patients and his front desk staff. Needless to say, the actions of his well-meaning front desk staff backfired, and the internet-savvy patient who experienced this incident posted a highly negative online review.

The incident in question concerns both the clinical and business side of today's medical practice, and the complex interrelationships among patients, physicians, outside service providers, and insurance companies. It's easy to see how opportunities for misunderstandings can arise in situations like this, and we can also identify with the stress everyone can feel when things don't happen as expected. For patients, choices between receiving needed care and paying unanticipated fees are among the most difficult aspects of the "patient care experience." It takes a calm, well-trained professional with excellent interpersonal skills to navigate the multiple demands of patients, their doctors, and outside organizations like insurance companies and diagnostic laboratories. The stage is set; here's the tale of "Mr. Smith" and his unexpected laboratory results. Again, as is the case everywhere in this book, Mr. Smith is not a real individual, nor is this simply the story of another individual whose name has been changed. It is an instructive story drawn from our broad experience working with physicians and other professionals seeking our financial management advice.

Our story begins when Mr. Smith, a young accountant in Los Angeles, comes to see Dr. Sally Franklin, our client, about a lingering stomach ailment. It's not serious, and though he hadn't missed any work, he thought it would be best to take time off and schedule an appointment to see what was going on. Dr. Franklin sees Mr. Smith, and after a few questions about his symptoms and the discovery that he is running a low fever, believes he may have contracted a bacterial infection that had been diagnosed among other patients from his part of the city in recent weeks. She prescribed a blood test and scheduled a call to follow up with Mr. Smith a week later, when the results would be in. This first day ended in a totally routine manner; blood was drawn, the test was ordered, and Mr. Smith's samples went out to the lab with the afternoon delivery. A week later, Dr. Franklin got the results, saw that in fact Mr. Smith had contracted the infection she suspected, and called him to come in for a brief visit and injection of antibiotics that were recommended for treatment. Again, at this second stage of Mr. Smith's experience, everything was going according to plan. He would come in for an appointment after work during the clinic's weekly Thursday evening sessions, two days after his conversation with Dr. Franklin.

That's when things began to unravel. Dr. Franklin's Thursday evening staff were new; she had just added this appointment time to her weekly schedule and none of her regular staff were available. They knew the basics, but didn't fully understand all the details for checking in patients and verifying their identities. Mr. Smith arrived, and when he checked in, he didn't receive the news he expected. Dr. Franklin's staff didn't bother to use standard methods for verifying patients' identity when they checked in. To be fair, they also didn't expect there to be two Mr. Smiths coming in for appointments that evening. The other Mr. Smith was due a bit later, and Dr. Franklin's staff grabbed his chart instead of the one for the patient in front of them. Reading this paperwork, the front desk receptionist called back to the chief administrator, and told Mr. Smith to sit down and wait until she called him back. It looked ominous, and it was; the receptionist was reading a file for a patient who had received a heart transplant some months before, and was coming in for a consultation about re-admission to the hospital for monitoring of a possible complication. Worse, the other Mr. Smith's health insurance had expired, so his chart was flagged for review by the administrator to see how this situation could be remedied. Otherwise, there would be significant out-of-pocket expenses for the patient, including a few services already provided, for which reimbursement had been denied.

The administrator came to the front desk, consulted with the receptionist, and called Mr. Smith into her office, explaining as respectfully as she could that she needed to help him get his insurance in order before continuing with the services scheduled for the evening's appointment. Naturally, since all he expected was a brief visit and an injection of antibiotics, Mr. Smith was alarmed. It took a few minutes of conversation with the administrator before it was clear there was something wrong, although the administrator wasn't sure what exactly was the source of the problem. She contacted the lab, thinking the problem may have started there, since the paperwork in front of her had all of the other Mr. Smith's lab work. Only after she returned to the front desk and saw the other Mr. Smith standing at the front desk with a confused look on his face did she realize what had happened. Eventually, Dr. Franklin's staff was able to regroup and match the correct patient records with the right Mr. Smith, and proceed with the care each of them needed to receive that evening. As an aside, Dr. Franklin's staff helped the other Mr. Smith re-activate his health insurance; it was a simple matter of his credit card being updated and the insurance company trying to charge the former card for his monthly premiums. Still, the Mr. Smith with the stomach bug was upset, and before he calmed down, posted a review about being told he needed hospitalization and might also need to pay several hundred dollars for lab work previously ordered on his behalf. Dr. Franklin certainly didn't need this sort of publicity. And it all resulted from the simple mistake of a new administrative employee being careless with patient records and not properly confirming every patient's identity.

"Not being too careful" is a general staff training lesson this incident might have for the business staff in Dr. Franklin's office. More specifically, following precise procedures for checking in patients is the specific thing her staff needed to re-emphasize with new employees. The larger issue for readers of this book, however, is the extent to which the smallest error can cause serious negative consequences. By the next day, both Mr. Smiths had received the care they were scheduled to receive, and by a few weeks later, both of them were healthy and going about their daily lives without restriction. "Our" Mr. Smith no longer had an intestinal infection, and the "other" Mr. Smith was admitted to the hospital for tests that ruled out any complications from his heart surgery. The "other" Mr. Smith even received additional support in maintaining his health insurance—an important concern given his potential need for expensive care related to his heart surgery. But all of this was known only to Dr. Franklin's Thursday evening staff and the two Mr. Smiths. Everyone else read the negative online review of her practice.

There are many organizations providing training for both the clinical and administrative staff who work in today's physicians' offices. These "customer service" advisors may have marketing issues that make them seem silly or off the mark in delivering training to medical personnel; a few of them cite corporations like large theme parks or international hotel chains as the source of their training courses. Many of our clients laugh when we mention these resources to them, and some dismiss them out of hand given these names. "I run a serious medical practice," they tell us. "We don't need any advice when it comes to taking care of people's health." This may be a valid objection, and there are training organizations that don't cite such distracting success stories as glowing examples of successful customer service. But objections to brand names are a minor detail; they should not be used as an excuse to ignore the need for customer service training for a physician's staff. And in today's medical care universe, there are no doubt many respected hospitals, community health centers, and other institutions that have implemented extensive customer training programs. Asking one of them is certainly a good place to start in looking for this valuable resource.

There are four key areas a practice should keep at the core of its staff training programs:

(1) **safety** for patients and staff alike;

(2) **quality** of care;

(3) **efficiency** operational procedures; and

(4) **positive customer/patient experiences**.

As readers will see throughout this book, we don't believe it is necessary for us to provide details about how to achieve each of these goals for a practice's customer service program. Introducing key principles is our goal; there are many different ways to successfully reach these goals;

matching a training program to the unique situation in each practice is an important way for physicians/business owners to find their own right answer. A few examples of the types of issues a good customer service training program can address follows. It's only a partial list, of course, but we're fairly confident more than a few of them will ring true for most readers.

Make sure someone answers the telephone promptly when a phone call comes to the office. Even when electronic answering systems are used to route calls to the proper department, care should be taken to provide for a human voice as soon as possible. Try to limit the number of times a caller should press a number in response to recorded questions, and by all means, don't disable the functionality of pressing "0" for operator.

When a human being does answer the phone, make sure this is done in a professional manner, and that the staff person on the phone pays close attention to the caller, and treats everyone as a respected and valued individual.

Make it easy for patients to set up appointments, and provide follow-up reminders for appointments. Simple telephone calls to patients a day or two before their scheduled appointments are a good way to start; other methods, including new technologies such as calendaring and texting, can also be used.

When patients come to the office, treat them with respect and make them feel welcome. Remember they may be nervous or apprehensive, and be patient if they are not as responsive or friendly as staff might like them to be. When possible, consider having front desk staff who speak other languages, so that patients whose native tongue is not English can also feel like this is "their" doctor's office too.

Provide patient follow-ups such as calling them a day after their exam or office visit to see how they're doing, confirm that prescriptions have been filled or that other recommendations are part of the patient's own follow-up programs, and to make sure they're feeling okay. I can guarantee it that when a phone call comes from a doctor to check on a patient, people tell others about their experience and this is what will differentiate one physician from others. Sometimes just one phone call is all it takes!

Speaking of languages, if your staff includes non-native English speakers, understand the importance of being considerate of patients when they communicate with each other. If office staff speak to each other in a "foreign" language in front of a patient, it may make that patient uncomfortable. In these situations, some individuals suspect that the staff are talking about them and trying to disguise what they are saying—even though in almost all cases, this is not the case. The importance of taking care to remember the heightened sensitivities patients bring to the office cannot be overestimated; even the most innocent behavior can be interpreted in a negative way by people in a state of anxiety.

The key to success in the training that physicians provide for their staff is in constant attention to the four general goals of good customer training, along with careful attention to detail as these lessons are executed. In addition to paying attention to these professional responsibilities, staff should also be aware that their behavior itself has an effect on the perceived quality of the service they—and the physician's office as a whole—are providing. The story of Dr. Smith's staff included examples of staff "going the extra mile" and helping a patient who needed assistance with his health insurance. Were it not for the mistake the front desk person had made, this would be the main point in a story about successful customer service by Dr. Smith's Thursday evening staff. Even so, this individual's willingness to help solve a problem outside of the responsibility of a physician's office is excellent work, and it also followed up the administrator's troubleshooting efforts to solve the confusion caused by the front desk receptionist's error. This type of attitude is sometimes interpreted as something people possess on their own, or as a skill that "cannot be taught." This is nonsense. All people can learn, and customer service is a skill that can be taught. Perhaps there are people who are naturally rude or without empathy for other people. When this is the case, the medical profession is certainly no place for them to work. Otherwise, the investment in staff training for both clinical and administrative functions always pays off.

Chapter 5

Advanced Planning—
What Does Health Care Reform Mean
for Physicians?

EARLIER, IN THE INTRODUCTION to this book, we mentioned the significance of changes coming to the health care system with the implementation of health care reform. While many of the new features of the Affordable Care Act (ACA) have been introduced since this law was passed by Congress, many doctors we know have been holding back, either because they were uncertain about whether the law might be overturned by Congress in subsequent years, or because they were unsure how to implement the changes the new law requires. Others were delaying making any adjustments in anticipation of implementation of the law because they were actually rooting for repeal. In any case, financial advisors like us can draw conclusions by watching the behavior of big businesses that have economic interests in the future of health care management in the United States. Big insurance companies and large hospitals are all preparing for the impact of health care reform. That's a clue. So should everyone else in the industry, including physicians who are employed by large corporations and those who own their own businesses.

That's not to say we are in a position to recommend specific actions physicians should take to prepare for the changes that are coming. But we can point to a large decision your practice will need to face at some point in the future: should you join an Affordable Care Organization (ACO)? It's a profound decision, and it's not a simple yes/no decision. There are many types of ACOs, and a number of key factors to consider in deciding whether or not your practice should decide to join one.

Health care reform will bring a number of difficult challenges for everyone in the business of caring for patients. There will be new ways of doing business, new partners in providing care, new regulations and administrative infrastructures, and—most of all—lots more paperwork (or, to be more accurate, pixelwork). Still, this brave new world will not be entirely unrecognizable. Note the names of the categories of advice for how to manage today's changing world of health care: "leadership and learning," "managing change," and "teamwork." Sound familiar? In fact, the ways financial advisors, management consultants, and other outside experts recommend approaching changes in the health care industry are similar to the strategies we recommend for managing any number of changes in business environments: new tax structures, new competitors entering the market, changing customer preferences, you name it...

The details are different in each of these challenges, as they always are. But the same basic types of financial planning still apply: (1) manage risks; (2) accumulate wealth; and (3) evaluate and select ways to "fine tune" your activities through advanced planning techniques and tools. And always ask for help. Other physicians will certainly be in the same boat. They're going to have relevant experiences in making these changes themselves, and may also be able to recommend advisors and consultants who can provide support for some of the larger "details" like adjusting your practice's EMRs or understanding exactly how the risks and rewards of keeping people out of the hospital will be measured. Your management team will also be a valuable resource in the coming months and years; share these challenges with them, and, when necessary, invest in education and training programs to help increase their knowledge and skill base. Strengthen relationships with allied organizations, and develop strong communication channels. You won't be able to manage these relationships from the top anymore. Practice owners should continue to talk to other practice owners and the CEOs of larger organizations to be sure; these bonds can never be ignored. But your nurses will need to talk to the nurses in your partner health care institutions; your physician assistants will need to know their peers in collaborating organizations as well. So will your administrative, finance, and billings departments, not to mention your IT people. Teamwork will be the rule in the future of health care, and this means becoming part of a team that goes far beyond the walls of your individual practice.

Within your practice, there will still be the need to pay attention to daily challenges and changes. People in your billings department should remain constantly vigilant for changes in medical insurance coverage and what these mean for receiving payments; even with global payments, there will still be new rules about eligibility for care, reimbursement rates, payment schedules, and timeliness of filing claims and reports. These can and will affect a practice's income. More important, these changes may affect a practice's continuing ability to retain current patients or accept new ones.

And don't forget your patients. They'll be struggling with the new rules and regulations of health care reform as well. Many of them will be happy with the new and extended benefits these changes bring them, but not all of them will know how to make the new system work to their best advantage. This is a great area for a creative medical practice to innovate. It's not yet clear how the relationship between patients and their insurance companies may change, and it may take a while for health care reform to change things at this level of the health care system. But the changes health care reform will bring to your practice will certainly bring more questions from your patients about what health care reform means to them. It's an opportunity to engage them in how to become more responsible for managing their own health. Education for how to live a healthier life at home will only increase as part of the services you provide. Take this challenge and make it a core element of the care your practice provides. It's something every member of your team can do, starting with the physician and continuing to every member of your clinical, support, and administrative teams.

One of the physicians we know—someone who worked in a community health center for many years before setting up her own private practice—remembers similar changes that happened during the early days of her work in community care. People in the neighborhood were wary of going to the health center, because they didn't want to be treated by medical students or residents completing their clinical training. They wanted to see a "real" doctor. At the time, she was just finishing her training herself, so she felt the sting of this skepticism from people she was trying to help. Over time, though, she recalled that the patients eventually "came around" when teams of doctors, nurses, and other providers visited patients in their homes and got to know their patients and their patients' families. There were bonds of trust that developed once people saw that other providers—not just doctors—cared about them, and could provide services, care, and information that helped keep them healthy. Nurses who were initially part of this larger team were soon welcome when they came back by themselves. Non-clinical staff who could follow up with issues related to appointments, referrals to other community organizations, and even insurance companies were appreciated for the ways they made health care easier for patients to navigate, and for the support they provided wherever they worked—either in home visits to support nurses, on the telephone before and after these visits, or when the patients came to visit the health center itself.

This lesson from community health centers in the 1970s applies in many ways to the changes health care reform is bringing to every physician and provider today. Teamwork, and a focus on the patient by every member of the team, is a good way to build the foundation necessary to achieve both the spirit and the letter of the goals health care reform is designed to achieve: healthier people, and healthier communities, needing less acute or inpatient care because they're taking better care of themselves. These are challenges you can share. There will be a number of "quality improvement" aspects to the new system, and a few of them will include opportunities for providers to contribute constructive criticism and suggest changes to how care is delivered, and how quality is measured. Don't be afraid to find these forums when you believe positive changes can be made. Remember that when everyone is learning, everyone is also a teacher.

Most of all, be ready for the new title health care reform will bring to you, regardless of whether you own your own private practice, are one of several physicians in a medical group, or are the head of a department in a large hospital or medical school. Forget "private practitioner," "department head," or even "chief of medicine." Aspire to any of these titles if you like, and keep them for old time's sake or marketing purposes, or for prestige with your peers. The new title you want to be sure is more important to you than any of them is this:

"Team Leader."

PART THREE
BUSINESS OWNER FINANCIAL PLANNING

Chapter 6

MANAGING RISK– BUSINESS INSURANCE PROTECTION NEEDS

IN PART TWO OF THIS BOOK, we introduced financial and practice management concepts that are specific to a physician's practice. The risk management, wealth accumulation, and advanced planning tools and techniques we've seen so far apply to the unique world of providing patient care, and to the business and support activities a practice needs to put in place to make a practice successful. Old ways of doing business were reviewed to sort out what remains relevant in today's world of health care reform, and to move on from procedures and habits that are no longer reliable. We also looked at the impact of changes coming from the larger world, and the pressures that may drive today's small, independent practices into parts of larger, comprehensive organizations designed to keep whole communities healthy, even if there is no fundamental change in the need to do most of this work one patient at a time.

At several times during our discussion of how physicians can best manage their practices and the financial health of these businesses in a changing world, we talked about how many of our recommendations were really the application of general business advice into the unique world of patient care. This third part of our book will take a more in-depth look at these "tried and true" techniques and tools many small businesses use to be successful, regardless of the specific industry in which they operate. Perhaps readers of this book will use their imaginations and creativity to think of new ways to apply this general knowledge beyond the specific recommendations we included in our previous chapters.

MANAGING THE RISKS THAT COME WITH PROVIDING PATIENT CARE

Doctors who run their own practices, or those who are members of a larger practice group are small business managers too, and the same financial planning and management recommendations that apply to other small business owners apply to physicians as well. The previous chapter's advice about marketing, risk management, and the delivery of quality care are themselves adaptations of these more general business principles to the world of caring for patients. Creating a welcoming and supportive physical environment in the waiting area and patient care rooms, establishing customer service standards and training programs, developing a solid marketing plan, and implementing financial controls and management are all taken from the techniques all successful businesses use to navigate the challenges of any rapidly changing industry. Even the need to monitor all the developments as health reform moves forward and global changes come to physicians' income streams and relationships with other health care organizations, insurance companies, and government agencies are "standard operating procedure" for wise small business owners in general.

These general principles can create their own kind of safe harbor for medical practice owners as they manage their way through uncertain times. Planning for one's financial future as a small business owner doesn't mean focusing on the changes within a particular industry alone. Physicians trying to keep up with the demands health care reform is bringing to their practices understand how easy it can be to become distracted by constant and conflicting "notices" from multiple sources. Successful management in time of change requires the application of broad tools and strategies to take advantage of every opportunity for managing income streams, keeping financial and other assets as secure as possible, maintaining morale and professional satisfaction for the physician and his/her staff, and protecting the personal independence that small business ownership brings. This third part of the book introduces some of these concepts as they apply to the management of risks, protection of assets and income streams, and compliance with the legal and regulatory requirements all small business owners face.

As discussed earlier in this book, every business has to deal with government regulations. Many small business owners are not aware of all of these needs; some of them have learned the hard way (i.e. too late) about the insurance coverage they require. Note that every state has its own rules and regulations about insurance coverage, including both types of coverage and minimum levels of protection. In the interest of keeping this book focused on big picture issues—and also in keeping its length under 1,000 pages—we are not going to describe the individual insurance requirements for each of the fifty states in this book. To illustrate some of our recommendations, we will use the state of California as an example of what states might require. Readers should consult tax and legal advisors in their home states to determine their specific business insurance coverage needs. Even better, they should seek the advice of a properly licensed and qualified insurance professional who is familiar with the requirements of his or her state.

THE FIRST TOOL: GENERAL LIABILITY INSURANCE

General liability insurance provides a business's basic first type of coverage. It protects the business itself, and the business owner, from paying losses awarded to consumers or business associates for a variety of situations, including accidents on the business's property, harm claimed to be the result of an owner's negligence, or activity that may be in violation of certain regulations or the law. Note that this chapter deals with business liability insurance as it pertains to the general interests of a small business owner; it does not discuss the additional liability coverage (i.e. malpractice or HIPAA-related risks) recommended for physicians who manage their own practices. Liability insurance (also known as Commercial General Business Liability) protects a company's assets and pays for a number of obligations—medical costs, for example—that result if someone gets hurt on your property, or when property damages or injuries to others are caused by you or your employees. Liability insurance also covers the cost of your legal defense and any settlement or award should you be successfully sued. Typically these include compensatory damages, nonmonetary losses suffered by the injured party, and punitive damages.

General liability insurance can also protect you against any liability as a tenant if you cause damage to a property that you rent, such as by fire or other covered loss. Additionally, either as part of the basic policy or through the addition of "endorsements" to cover additional risks, it can also cover claims of false or misleading advertising, including libel, slander, and copyright infringement. As we've mentioned in other sections of this book, reviewing every insurance policy to determine what type of protection it actually provides is a key risk management responsibility. The definition of covered losses is one critical aspect of this review; just because a policy is entitled "general liability" doesn't mean its coverage is as general as a business owner might want or need. Among the other things to check are the limits on claims the policy will pay. These upper limits may be adequate when a policy is first purchased, but the acquisition of additional assets by a small business will require additional coverage. In other cases, insurance companies may change these coverage limits on their own, requiring adjustments to existing policies or perhaps purchasing additional policies to meet risk management goals.[1]

A RELATED RESOURCE: PROFESSIONAL LIABILITY INSURANCE

In Part One of this book, we've already discussed the importance of malpractice insurance for physicians, whether they are small business owners or salaried employees. Malpractice insurance is vital for physicians, and many insurance companies include more general "professional liability" coverage in the policies they sell to physicians that cover malpractice—the most important professional liability in this case. But this may not be adequate coverage for all of the "business risks" physicians' practices face. There are additional requirements for professional liability coverage for small business owners beyond those that are specific to medical practice; these include coverage in the event of lawsuits or litigation related to non-clinical operations of the business itself. Physicians cannot

1 https://www.sba.gov/blogs/general-business-liability-insurance-how-it-works-and-what-coverage-right-you

assume that their malpractice insurance coverage provides protection in the event of contractual disputes, or contested ownership of intellectual property or other intangible assets, or relationships with clients and prospective clients, sometimes defined as "good will." Insurance salesmen may tell prospects that the malpractice insurance they offer covers a broad range of professional liability risks and is the only policy a doctor will need for these purposes. However, this may not be the case when a policy is thoroughly reviewed. Potential losses from non-clinical professional liability lawsuits are a leading cause of financial risks that can be mitigated through the purchase of professional liability insurance that matches the needs of a physician, particularly one who owns a practice/small business. It's a vital insurance product physicians need to include in their overall risk management strategy.

Doctors should be informed about which of these policies will be more appropriate for their type of practice, and should also be informed about what may be excluded in these policies, including the effects of different corporation names, different business structures such as partnerships or LLCs, and the coverage required for practices that include the services of other medical professionals who may be employed or affiliated with the doctor's practice. Many doctors have partners in their practices, and if these partners are Physician Assistants (Pas), Nurse Practitioners (NPs), Nurses, and other professionals, their malpractice insurance may cover risks as fully as the physician partner intends or needs. Further, some policies cover multiple physicians, some cover corporations and extend this corporate coverage to all partners/owners, and others require listing every individual covered. As physicians make adjustments to their practice, they should bring questions about coverage for all professionals involved in the practice (and related questions) to their insurance brokers for evaluation.

Based on their advice, the physician can then make proper adjustments.

THE IMPORTANCE OF EMPLOYEE PRACTICES LIABILITY INSURANCE

Physicians must also be aware of what is excluded from these policies. There are certain acts and liabilities that may not be covered under one particular policy, and doctors may be required to purchase a different type of insurance to protect the practice against these perils. For example, criminal acts may not be covered by some malpractice policies; while cyber liability or HIPAA violations may not be covered by professional liability policies. Employment practices liability, also known as EPL, may also be excluded or may not be covered under a physician's general liability or professional malpractice policies. (Insurance covering this type of liability is known as EPL I.) Physicians and medical groups are encouraged to thoroughly review these options and understand the risks and the cost associated with not having such policies. In today's economy many medical providers are being targeted for hacking and cyber attacks, and patients whose medical records have been compromised are able to sue the provider maintaining their confidential information. Physicians and business owners are urged to look into these policies, not only to protect themselves in the event of potential hacks and theft of patient information from malicious outsiders, but also to protect themselves from inadvertent mistakes they or their employees may make.

Let's look a bit more into the details of EPL I. Employee liability has always been a concern in the management of many businesses—including those in the medical field—and it is becoming more and more of a concern as employees in many states—whether they are current or past employees, "disgruntled" or not—are able to file claims for a variety of legal violations, including wrongful termination, sexual harassment, breach of employment contract, or discrimination based on age, race, or sexual orientation. These claims may be filed against the owner him/herself, or against the business owner's management employees; in either case, the business is liable. Most general liability and virtually all malpractice policies do not provide such protection, and the business owner/physician bears the responsibility for researching and evaluating the costs associated with adding this very important protection to the practice's insurance package. This coverage can help prevent an enormous headache; without it, the enormous amount of distraction these lawsuits bring can damage any business. Even worse, the potential out-of-pocket expense of navigating these lawsuits, and the risk of paying large settlements to employees who win them, can ruin a business entirely. EPL I may not be a well-understood type of insurance protection, but it is vital. These types of policies should be researched, negotiated, and purchased with the help of a qualified, licensed, and—again, most important—*experienced* insurance professional.

WORKERS' COMPENSATION INSURANCE

Workers' compensation, employee medical and dental insurance, disability insurance, and other coverage often included in employee benefit packages are mentioned earlier in Part Two (for their relevance to physician practices), and below in Part Four (to introduce considerations individuals and families may need to take into account). A financial advisor who is properly licensed for commercial insurance, and a broker who has experience in a physician's home state can be valuable partners in finding the best policy structures and coverage levels for these insurance products. This experience is vital; physicians should make every effort to engage experienced advisors when selecting employee benefit-related insurance. Many insurance advisors, even those with professional licenses, do not understand the intricacies of commercial and business insurance. This is particularly true with workers' compensation coverage, since it may extend vital coverage to people a small business owner might believe are "outside" of his or her business, including consultants, contractors, and even delivery people. Just because you have an independent contractor working for you doesn't mean you're off the hook and do not need workers' compensation insurance. Physicians and business owners need to carefully check the regulations for their city and state requirements for coverage of themselves, their employees, and for any independent contractors through workers' compensation, disability, and other insurance policies.

Workers' compensation insurance is often understood to provide coverage for medical expenses associated with on-the-job injuries. In fact, as we have seen in our earlier discussions, it can also provide income to replace lost wages while a worker is disabled, or other benefits. When a physician is acting in the role of small business owner, these benefits become an important concern beyond the cost of premiums for these insurance policies themselves. The level of benefits provided to employees also becomes important, in terms of the value a good benefits package has in recruiting and retaining quality employees, and also in ensuring the business complies with state and other government requirements for minimum coverage of employees if these exist.

Finally, here is something to remember: group workers' compensation policies may not cover business owners. They only cover employees and independent contractors. As a result, there are often some counter-intuitive ways a physician may need to structure group and individual disability policies to provide adequate coverage for employees and him/herself. It is also critical to pay attention to the sequence in which these plans must be put into place—in order to implement a risk management program that provides employees with basic coverage and adds the additional benefits a physician and his/her family and business partners will need in the event of a disabling illness or injury.

LIFE INSURANCE: MORE THAN YOU MIGHT THINK

Life insurance also plays a big part in a business continuation situation, especially for those physicians who have multiple partners and partnerships. When there is lack of cash or liquidity in the business, life insurance can play a great part in the funding mechanism for such an agreement. Without getting too far into the specifics of how life insurance can help with business continuation, the general concept is this: if a business has inadequate cash reserves to pay the heirs of a deceased partner for the share of the business they have inherited, the continued existence of the business can be threatened. A life insurance policy owned by the business that insures the life of one or all partners is a way this cash can be acquired in the event of the premature death of any single partner.

In addition to the life insurance policy itself, there needs to be a corresponding agreement in place that acknowledges the purpose of the policy and directs how its proceeds will be used to purchase the deceased partner's share from his/her heirs. This combination helps protect both the family of the deceased partner and the surviving partners to maintain their financial interests without disrupting or terminating the ongoing operation of the business itself.

This planning process is extremely difficult and has to be done by trained professionals, who may include an estate planning attorney, plus a qualified financial professional who understands the best way to design and implement a life insurance solution for business continuation purposes. More information on this and other advanced financial planning tools and resources can be found below in Chapter 12 of this book.

ADDITIONAL EXTERNAL RISKS: THE IMPACT OF POTENTIAL NEW REGULATIONS

Finally, in addition to risk management strategies aimed at the above-referenced dangers that are internal to a physician's practice/small business, there are also a large number of external risks associated with state and federal government regulations. Changing the way a practice does business in response to new and changing regulations—many of which are likely to be revised on an increasingly frequent basis—is costly in and of themselves. But failure to comply can be far worse in terms of penalties and fines, and additional exposure to lawsuits that may not even be on a physician's radar. These regulations cover the way care is provided, patient confidentiality, and notifications to patients and even the general public. No doctor can be expected to keep up with all of them, nor can all but the largest of administrative support staff teams. A corresponding disadvantage for small practices is that this large organization will adapt these primary rules and regulations to fit its own standard operating procedures.

Staying ahead of changing regulations and government policies means opening up new channels of communication with these agencies, but also with other providers and physician practices. You can't influence what you don't know. Attending meetings and conferences, and establishing informal relationships with other health care institutions, will be useful techniques in the new world of health care reform. These may or may not be responsibilities some physicians want to accept. This is fine, as long as someone they trust in their practice takes them on. The practice as a whole needs to be represented and recognized as a member organization with its own interests that need to be respected or at least considered. Internal networking is definitely a new cost of doing business in today's changing world of health care. And there are few business management techniques as old and as valuable as networking.

HOW THESE "OLD" TOOLS APPLY TO THE NEW WORLD OF HEALTH CARE REFORM

Again, while the matter of securing electronic medical records (EMRs) was covered in Part Two of this book, it is also worth reminding readers that the insurance used to manage this sort of risk is in fact based on general business insurance products. So is the advice financial professionals like us give to physicians in these cases. Like any business owner with sensitive online data in the office (in other words, like everyone), physicians and medical professionals cannot use unsecure e-mail services; these make a business vulnerable to hacking and potential legal action from customers, vendors, business partners, and others whose data may be stored in the business's electronic management information systems. We recommend that everyone seek the advice of professionals in the field of data security to ensure that their electronically-stored information is secure from hacking via their e-mail system, and that the office's data storage servers are secure as well, as a second line of defense. Furthermore, the physician's staff must be trained to take extra precautions when faxing sensitive patient information, and to make sure that fax numbers are correct when documents are being shared using this technology. Inadvertent faxing of sensitive information can be just as serious as leaving electronic data vulnerable to hacking. Human error is still the largest single source of exposure to professional liability and malpractice claims, and the best way to limit these claims includes the three elements of:

- Ensuring that communications and data storage systems are secure from hacking and intrusion;
- Purchasing adequate professional liability, malpractice, and other insurance to cover potential claims; and
- Training staff in ways they can avoid risky behavior and activities in their daily work.

We cannot underestimate the importance of all of these strategies in managing the wide array of risks—those that are associated with technology, and those that result from mistakes made by human beings—that are present in the daily operation of today's medical practices; while these "old" methods of risk management apply to many other businesses, the risks for physicians are larger than they are for almost anyone else.

Finally, because so many of these "old" ways of doing business will always apply, even in the new world of health care reform, we can't end this or any chapter of our book without reminding readers of the importance of finding and working with a qualified and experienced financial advisor. In many circumstances physicians will find new and confusing, there are relevant examples of successful change management in other industries. Professionals with insights from their experience working with other clients facing similar challenges can provide the best defense in these circumstances.

Chapter 7

WEALTH ACCUMULATION– CASH MANAGEMENT CONCERNS FOR SMALL BUSINESSES

MANAGING CASH FLOW is a crucial responsibility for all small business owners. There are a number of strategies people use to accomplish this, but one of my favorite recommendations is the design of a plan that matches larger goals with the allocation of funds to support them. In other words, once a physician/business owner has identified key priorities for the future, each of these priorities should be matched with a separate financial plan for accomplishing it. For example, different funds (or bank accounts, or stock portfolios, or any other preferred financial instrument) should be created to handle day-to-day expenses, business-related investments and other growth needs, or emergency funds to handle unexpected crises. And once a plan with matching funds to support its key elements is in place, my next-favorite recommendation is to not do things on one's own. Hiring an adequate number of office staff to create a business/administrative department is essential, no matter how small a business might be.

Physicians may be small business owners in order to realize their personal goals of being free from the pressures and priorities that come with employment by a large hospital or other institution. But they rarely if ever want to see the responsibilities of keeping this small business healthy get in the way of providing care to their patients. A trusted administrator or business manager is a great first step in making sure a physician's financial plans become a reality. This individual should be seen as a partner in key business and financial decisions, including the physician's overall financial plan and the steps needed to reach key milestones and overall goals. And, in order to keep the plan on track, this business manager will need to be trusted with responsibility for many business details. Managing billings, employees, their compensation and benefits packages, equipment, and accounts payable will likely require skills and time beyond what a physician/practice owner is willing to commit.

If a practice is large enough, even the business manager may require additional help in order to handle all of these details. For example, in today's rapidly-changing world of health insurance, with third-party revenue becoming a mix of reimbursements and global payments, billing staff are vital to prevent a loss of income. Time in processing claims is also money. Many payments from government agencies and private health insurance companies are reduced based on the amount of time between provision of service and date of billing; rapid filing of claims equals higher reimbursements. In many cases, this equation becomes the strong rationale for hiring staff necessary to keep things flowing smoothly; staff salaries are often exceeded by the additional revenue their timely work brings in.

DEBT: WHEN IS THE RIGHT TIME TO BORROW?

We should also talk about situations in which implementing elements of a financial or business plan simply cannot wait for the accumulation of enough funds from ongoing operations to support them. Hiring staff to file timely claims with government and private insurers is one example. Others might be the purchase of medical equipment that will allow the practice to increase its patient population through the offer of additional services. Another might be some of the marketing and office environment investments we discussed in Part Two of this book. In these cases, seeking a loan from a bank or financial institution may be the best way to proceed. And while this is similar to advice we will offer for managing one's individual finances in Part Four, it is even more important for a small business to evaluate the needs and opportunities for debt financing, and, if debt is already in place, to review current loans to see if anything should be paid off or refinanced. This includes business loans, refinanced mortgage loans, or even a line of credit to fund some of the projects that will bring additional revenue or expense savings into the practice. In these cases, in addition to trusting the practice's business manager to evaluate various options, it may also be wise to consult with a financial advisor and a CPA to be sure the best method is selected. Some loans may be tax favored and some may not.

It's worth noting that, in some cases, despite their presence in most counts of America's high-wealth individuals, some physicians can't get a specific type of loan such as a business loan, and others don't wind up securing the right kind of loan when they need cash for business expansion or short-term operational needs related to the cash flow irregularities inherent in their relationships with public and private third-party payers.

In such instances, doctors need to shop around for the best possible loan for the specific cash need they wish to finance; too often, they go to the nearest bank and take what that banker offers. New physicians may be surprised to find that, in some cases, the large amount of debt they carry from their medical education makes them a bad candidate for business loans. It's a painful reality, but it is also one that can be overcome by finding a banker who understands the profession and is willing to invest in a long-term relationship. In fact, the concept of long-term relationships with financial professionals is something we financial advisors like almost as much as we like risk management. These relationships also invariably pay off in the end.

Like we have done in many other cases in this book and in our relationships with our physician clients, we enjoy illustrating what we mean by telling stories from previous experiences with doctors seeking our help. In this case, we're reminded of a young doctor (again, a fictional character based on several experiences with many different clients) who wanted to be a general practitioner—a selfless and noble decision we thought was wonderful—but who was having difficulty setting up his practice. He had found a good banker (we knew the banker and agreed she was a good choice), had set up a reasonable line of credit to deal with the difference between his "certain" monthly obligations like rent and support staff salaries and the "uncertain" monthly revenue from Medicare, Medicaid, and some of his private insurer partners. A few months into his second year of operations, he decided to expand his practice, and did a thorough analysis of the costs of additional equipment and staff vs. the income he expected from this expansion. In fact, his projections were right on target. Everything went according to his plan. Everything, that is, except for the terms of the loan he used to finance his expansion. He knew he would go into debt for an initial period of time before new revenue came in to cover increased operational costs and to completely repay the debt he would incur from buying the equipment he needed. His estimate for this was eighteen months, which is a relatively short repayment period, and he was confidently on track to make this deadline when his banker called him in to talk about a serious issue.

Our young doctor had failed to consult his banker, thinking this was a small matter, and confident that he wasn't incurring any risk serious enough to be of concern. So he was surprised—panicked, actually—to receive an ominous letter from his banker. He called us immediately, before talking with his banker, to ask us to explain the problem he was in, and to ask for our advice in getting out of it.

When our young doctor friend arrived at our offices, he explained the situation, and his surprise that there was any problem. The cost of the equipment he purchased required him to borrow a relatively low amount compared to his bank loan's limit, and he thought the eighteen-month break-even point was reasonable. We agreed that he had made a prudent business decision, but it was easy for us to see the mistake he had made; he had simply failed to realize that the loan he chose to use for buying his equipment was the same line of credit he had set up at the time he opened his practice. It needed to be cleared to a $0 balance for a thirty-day period every year, and his eighteen-month payback schedule didn't account for this requirement. He simply overlooked this clause in his loan agreement, and unintentionally violated it. Luckily, we knew the banker well, and our young client was a responsible businessman. In relatively short order, we helped him arrange for a proper loan package with the bank. They were able to issue a term loan for the equipment he purchased, with the same eighteen-month payback period he had created when he did these calculations for himself. And they kept his line of credit intact, although they did reduce the total amount of both loans to the former limit of his line of credit, agreeing to reset the line to its original amount upon successful repayment of his term loan. This was a bit of a harsh lesson from our banker friend in our opinion, but we went along with it in order to respect her opinion that a lesson needed to be learned. Our young doctor didn't mind; he was never going to need the money temporarily unavailable to him via his line of credit in any case.

And so the happy lesson learned was to develop strong relationships with your banker from the earliest stages of your business's operations as possible, and to consult with this person as a valued colleague in managing your business. Our young banker could have avoided this entire matter—brief though it was—by telling his banker he wanted to expand his business, and showing her the excellent break-even calculations he had made before moving forward with his plan. The larger lesson for everyone, including our young doctor client, is that there are many different types of loans available, and that matching these types of loans to the reasons why a physician might need cash are worth investigating before choosing the loan that works best. In this case, our doctor assumed a loan was a loan, and as long as he could repay it, there should be no issue. Once he realized his mistake, he was lucky to be in a position to correct that error and continue to operate his business. And actually, the interest rate for his equipment loan turned out to be lower than the one for his line of credit. In retrospect, he could have explored a number of similar loans, even the financing programs offered by the manufacturer of the equipment he purchased, to find even more favorable terms. Or he could have leased the equipment and helped reduce the risk of carrying assets that might become obsolete in a relatively short time, allowing him to update his equipment when new features were added. We could have helped him do all of this, if he had asked.

Debt should always be evaluated in the context of the purposes for which it will be incurred, and by looking at other possible revenue streams. For example, the physician who owns a practice with high receivables may be eligible for a different type of loan or financial product than a different business that also has irregular cash flows, but doesn't have as high a level of receivables. In these cases, loans secured against liquid or fixed assets can provide the funding that is required. And remember that not all business goals are equally time-sensitive. While debt financing may make sense for investments in new equipment or additional staff, it may not be as beneficial to borrow in order to meet other financial objectives. Emergency funds, for example, may be worth covering with a combination of cash reserves and insurance, particularly if a practice has developed strong risk-management strategies and insurance coverage may cover some of these unexpected events. A line of credit may also be a good alternative for handling the financial consequences of smaller business emergencies, although, as we saw with our young doctor, the requirements financial institutions often put in place, such as "clearing the line," need careful evaluation. Sometimes, lines of credit can be valuable parts of a total financial plan to cover expanded operations; for example, they may cover temporary increases in the irregularities of payments as third-party reimbursements catch up with new billings. No matter what the reason for borrowing, care must always be taken to make sure the right loan product is matched with the financial needs of any new project.

Planning for and using debt financing is a good example of the importance of a physician's relationship with individuals and businesses outside of the practice. A financial institution that understands the nature of the physician's business, and the opportunities and risks it faces, can be helpful in the evaluation and selection of the "right" kind of debt financing.

It's their business to make successful loans, and they can often select the right product, or, in some cases, structure loans in creative ways to match projects their clients want to fund. Longer-term repayment terms can be negotiated for equipment purchases and installation, while shorter-term loans or even use of a line of credit can be used if new income streams will be available more quickly. Bankers appreciate being included in discussions of how funds will be used, and if possible, doing this can increase the likelihood of a loan being designed in the most favorable way possible.

CREATIVE FINANCING: BEYOND THE BANKS

Banks and financial institutions aren't the only places a physician's practice can turn to when considering a loan. A wide variety of government agencies—state, federal, and even local—plus a few charitable foundations or even academic institutions, can sometimes offer loans at favorable terms for medical projects that are designed to increase access to care among populations they believe are under-served. This is particularly true for practices located in urban neighborhoods, and also for practices located in rural areas. It's sometimes surprising to learn that health care is included in a number of programs that seem outside of the field. Anti-poverty programs may determine that disadvantaged individuals need good health care in addition to education and employment training, to avoid the distractions that come with being sick or needing to navigate difficulties in the health care system. The Department of Agriculture may see the need for health care among seasonal farm workers or residents of rural areas in general as needs worthy of programs to fund access to care. Professional financial advisors like us know these programs exist; however, we may not be the best source of information on specific opportunities for loans or grants. Networking with other health care organizations is probably the best way for a practice to look into these opportunities.[1]

Overall, however, this type of financing is a good option if a practice is already committed to serving patients who are included in the "target populations" government agencies define to be in need of additional health care resources. And in many cases, collaboration with a community health center or other nonprofit organization may be required in order to meet goals larger than the provision of health care alone. For example, an urban anti-poverty program will likely require such additional services as employment and training programs, or behavioral health services in addition to access to primary care. Rural initiatives may include transportation services in addition to other human service programs. Some of these initiatives may also include research components and other activities some physicians might find interesting as a way to give back to the community while increasing their patient population. Other physicians might find these additional program elements to be a distraction.

The point is that these loan programs may be a great idea if they support business plans that are already in place. Trying to qualify for a loan by adding new services, or by marketing existing services to a new patient population, is usually not a good idea. In our experience, we've worked with a number of private practitioners and even the administrators of large hospitals who embarked on new programs of care only to find unpleasant surprises after they've taken the leap. Medicare and Medicaid funding are almost always part of the revenue streams from programs aimed at increasing access to services among disadvantaged populations; and while

---

1 Source for Department of Agriculture Funding: http://www.usda.gov/documents/RURAL_HEALTH_CARE_AND_HEALTH_INSURANCE.pdf

health care reform may change this, current reimbursable rates from these sources are normally lower than those from other insurance payers. In a few of these cases, health care organizations that made decisions to enter into programs that increase access to care have been disappointed by this choice. Some of those who made these decisions based on financial considerations quickly determined that the lower per capita revenue from these new patients didn't meet their revenue requirements for new patients in general. And then they found themselves in the awkward and embarrassing situation of either choosing to continue losing money by remaining in these new ventures, or canceling their participation in them and risking the bad publicity and other negative consequences of backing out of commitments to provide care to people in need.

In closing, there are a number of financial planning tools, products, and strategies that physicians can adapt from those that are popular with small businesses in a variety of other industries. Every small business owner wants to maximize profits, minimize risks, serve real customer needs, and maintain a happy and productive work force. Even as these concepts are adapted to meet the unique realities of organizations providing health care, they are important for a physician practice to discover, evaluate, and implement in selected cases. But business decisions based on financial considerations alone are rarely a good idea if they don't fit an owner's business model, or the mission of an organization that has its origin in considerations beyond maintaining a margin between revenue and expense.

Doctors have always been seen as an important part of any community's sense of identity, just like good school systems, and a vibrant downtown area with retail and cultural attractions. On one hand, doctors are members of a "professional class" including lawyers, bankers, and others. People tend to move to communities where there are strong networks of these professionals, particularly those who have a sense of service to the community. Doctors almost always qualify for this status by simply being doctors, but a practice that identifies itself as one that is concerned about community health beyond its interest in dollars and cents can build strong relationships with other leaders in town. This is an important element in finding the non-financial rewards of being a physician in any community, and we encourage all medical providers to look for opportunities for this sort of involvement. These networks also "pay off" in the sense that, over time, opportunities come to those who are willing to share their time and resources with others. It may seem odd to see these recommendations in a book about financial management for physicians, and particularly in a chapter of that book about wealth accumulation. But of course, that depends on what you define as "wealth."

Chapter 8

ADVANCED PLANNING– EMPLOYEE BENEFITS AND HUMAN RESOURCE ISSUES

BUSINESS ADVISORS FROM ALL walks of life always rank the importance of people in assuring the success of any venture. Business school libraries and the business sections of book stores and online retailers are full of these volumes. Much of this advice can seem obvious, or in some cases, repetitive. But there are a few reasons why human resource issues are so vital in the management of a physician's office. These include the primary role clinical staff play in delivery of medical services, and the equally important role administrative and support staff play in the delivery of quality customer service. There are few other industries in which employees play such a vital role. Good staff, well-trained in the provision of care and the requirements of managing a successful practice, can be critical to business success. On the other hand, staff—those who either lack motivation, or training, or support—can also break a medical practice. Because of these considerations, strategies for managing staff at all levels of a doctor's office are critically important. This chapter will outline some of the more effective techniques for doing that.

GROUP HEALTH INSURANCE

One of the most prevalent employee benefits provided by American employers, this type of insurance is undergoing significant changes to the coverage it provides and the way people obtain and maintain that coverage. The Patient Protection and Affordable Care Act of 2010 (ACA) requires that every American have health insurance, eliminates restrictions on coverage due to pre-existing conditions, extends coverage for dependent children to age twenty-six, and mandates many other minimum standards for what it calls "ACA compliant plans." Other changes that may be less popular include (in many cases) higher premiums, and premiums based on residential zip codes. Some plans do not provide coverage by hospitals and doctors through restrictive network arrangements determined by the insurance company offering the plan; other plans may not be accepted by doctors and providers themselves.

Plans in effect prior to the ACA's effective date are referred to as "grandfathered plans." These plans are no longer available for people who seek new medical insurance today; however, the law has allowed people who have these older grandfathered plans to be able to keep them. What we have seen most recently is that the rates of increases in premiums are much higher with these grandfathered plans than they are with the new ACA plans. One reason may be that they do provide access to a different form of network of physicians and hospitals, but these also may be changing depending on future decisions made by the health care industry and federal government. Many ACA compliant plans are offered in "tiers," based on the number of services covered, different levels for co-payments and deductibles, and monthly cost. Companies with more than fifty, and in some cases more than one hundred employees may be required to offer ACA compliant group health insurance to their employees. It is important to note that many of these laws are changing rapidly, and the contents of this information in this book may be changing. There are also a number of other requirements governing coverage for part-time vs. full-time employees.

Based on their size (2–50 employees; 51–100 employees; more than 100 employees), companies must comply with different requirements for offering coverage; the plans themselves may also differ based on these same criteria. Companies offering coverage may continue to pay a portion of the costs of these plans, and may do so pre-tax through their payroll system. Small businesses under the fifty-employee limit may refer their employees to their state exchange to purchase coverage as individuals (or, in cases where a state has no such exchange, through the federal exchange); individuals and their families may qualify for subsidies based on their annual income. Some low-income people will find coverage through Medicaid; this will vary from state to state. Now more than ever, a qualified human resources advisor is necessary to ensure compliance with necessary regulations and requirements in order to avoid penalties and potential violations.

The ACA has created open enrollment dates when people can enroll in a health insurance plan through a state/federal exchange. Small businesses may also purchase group health insurance for their employees through employer exchanges set up under the ACA. In some cases, people may qualify to enroll in a plan outside these dates, which is referred to as "Special Open Enrollments."

Finally, this may be seen by some as stating the obvious, but group health insurance should still be considered as a primary benefit to be offered to most employees. Regardless of coverage requirements that are part of the ACA, providing group health insurance is a vital tool in the recruitment and retention of quality employees. Most working people believe this is the next-most-important part of any compensation package, after wages or salaries. Failure to provide group health insurance may cost practices the additional expense of replacing experienced staff with new employees as people seek employment elsewhere with an organization providing group health insurance. A practice's human resource manager may need to comply with Department of Labor requirements and additional laws, some of which are extremely complicated. In some cases, this HR manager may require training and, ultimately, certification in order to provide information about benefits to a practice's employees.

GROUP DISABILITY AND LONG-TERM CARE INSURANCE

These plans are important ways to ensure the employees and their families are protected from unexpected accidents and/or sicknesses that may cause them to become unable to work and earn an income. Like other employee benefits, they help recruit and retain employees; benefits like this make them feel more able to ensure their financial security, and that of their families. Companies can offer group disability and long-term care insurance as part of a standard package for all employees, or they can make these benefits voluntary, with costs (or a portion of the costs) borne by the employees. In fact, coverage by most plans is typically paid by employees. Planning for how the costs of these plans will be paid is an important consideration. When premiums are paid by the employee as after-tax benefits, payments when a claim is made may be tax-free. If the employer pays such plans' premiums, benefits may be taxable when there is a claim. Group disability and long-term care plans are typically low in cost, but coverage may not be as extensive as is the case for individual plans. Long-term care plans are experiencing higher levels of claims, resulting in plan changes that are often restrictive in benefits or higher in costs. Some insurance companies are moving away from these plans as a result. Physicians who own their own practices should have the maximum amount of disability insurance possible, given what is likely to be a large amount of income that would need to be replaced in the event of an accident or illness.

It is also important to make sure that the difference between group disability insurance and individual disability insurance is taken into account with respect to this type of coverage. In many cases, a physician practice or other small business may offer group disability insurance that has limits on the dollar value of income they will provide to employees in the event of disability; this may also be expressed as a percentage of covered employees' salaries. By law, group plans must cover all policy holders equally; therefore these same limits will apply to the business owner as well as all employees. In these cases, the physician or business owner may consider purchasing an individual disability policy to cover the additional income that would be necessary to support the physician and his or her family in the event of a disabling event. In cases like this, care must be taken to manage the implementation of these plans in a proper sequence. Sometimes, if the group disability insurance is set up first, this may affect how much individual disability can be purchased later. However, there may be more flexibility and independent eligibility for claims when an individual disability policy is purchased first, before group insurance policies are put into place. Plans that are not implemented with these considerations in mind may not provide the protection a physician or business owner requires, no matter how much is paid in policy premiums. It is rec-ommended that these disability policies include the "Non-cancelable" and "Guaranteed Renewable" clauses. This means that the insurance company cannot raise the rates and only the insured/policy owner can cancel the policy. The definition of disability also is extremely important. Physicians need to ensure that the policy covers their own occupation, and that this definition is an adequate description in terms of coverage. These consid-erations are important, because disability benefits are typically paid when the insured is unable to work at his or her "current occupation."

Some physicians and other business owners should also consider having business overhead expenses coverage (BOE) in their disability plans, which will pay for the cost of running the office while they are out on disability. Covered expenses include such day-to-day items as payroll, insurance, rent, and perhaps funding to hire temporary staff to cover ser-vice delivery. Physicians who own and/or manage practices with a partner or partners might want to consider a buy/sell agreement with a disability insurance policy, and may even include a buy-out option, which can help manage an ownership transition in the event one of the partners becomes permanently disabled, or dies. Such agreements can ensure that the dis-abled partner, or the spouse and family of a deceased partner, will be able to live more easily and not have to deal with resulting financial uncertain-ties. The definition of disability is extremely important as well; working with a qualified insurance broker to make sure a policy will pay benefits for a broad range of possible disabilities is a vital element in structuring any disability insurance, whether it is a group or individual plan. In ad-dition, any buy/sell agreement or buy-out option must contain the same definition of disability as the insurance policy itself.

SECTION 125 AND CAFETERIA PLANS

Cafeteria plans are benefit plans an employer provides to employees under specific requirements of Section 125 of the Internal Revenue Code. They offer participants a choice of benefits, some of which can be received on a pre-tax basis. Cafeteria plans require that employees be offered the choice among at least one taxable benefit (cash is an example of this type of benefit) and one qualified benefit. A qualified benefit is defined by the IRS as one "that does not defer compensation and is excludable from an employee's gross income under a specific provision of the Code, without being subject to the principles of constructive receipt." Examples of qualified benefits include:

- Accident and health benefits (excluding certain medical savings accounts or long-term care insurance)
- Adoption assistance
- Dependent care assistance
- Group-term life insurance coverage
- Health savings accounts, including distributions to pay long-term care services

A cafeteria's written plan must specifically describe all benefits, establish rules for eligibility, and set the method through which these benefits are selected. A cafeteria plan may make benefits available to employees, their spouses, and dependents. It may also include former employees. Smaller employers may not be aware of these and other requirements associated with the provision and administration of cafeteria plans for their employees. Cafeteria plans allow certain benefits offered through an employer to be offered to employees on a pre-tax basis. In addition to these tax savings, cafeteria plans may also provide substantial savings when compared to the higher price employees might pay if they were to seek similar benefits on an individual basis, outside of a group plan.

When these plans are put into place, employers must follow very strict procedures to make sure their plans are compliant and are documented with the proper filings for state and federal governments. These filings are usually referred to as plan documents. Plan documents are required to clearly state what benefits are offered and who is eligible so that there is no discrimination.[1]

HUMAN RESOURCES CONSIDERATIONS AND COMPLIANCE

Labor laws are complex and getting more complicated every day. Physicians who are employers should prepare for compliance with these laws and regulations. Failing to do so will almost certainly have a negative effect on their practices; on the other hand, many labor laws can help employers protect themselves from a number of liabilities. A qualified human resources consultant can help a practice adapt to the latest requirements, and—equally important—inform employees about these rules and regulations in employee handbooks, in-office postings, and other publications. It is good practice to include regular performance reviews and staff training, with appropriate documentation in employee files. Other responsibilities of the employer include making sure that any benefits put into place are in compliance with federal and state anti-discrimination laws, and other state regulatory guidelines. These regulations are complex and they change on a frequent basis. Few employers, physicians or otherwise, are qualified to

---

1 http://www.irs.gov/Government-Entities/Federal,-State-&-Local-Governments/
FAQs-for-government-entities-regarding-Cafeteria-Plans

manage compliance with all human resource-related laws and regulations without the advice of a financial advisor with qualifications and experience in human resource management.

One example of recent changes that mean additional work by a practice's human resources office is the requirement that employees receive personal summary of benefits coverage (SBC) documentation, listing all medical, dental, and other benefits, whether they are offered as stand-alone plans or as part of a cafeteria plan. The person in a physician's business office responsible for human resources should become familiar with these new requirements. Some other compliance requirements may include requirements for hiring or terminating an employee, and how the employer may or may not perform these responsibilities. Others include notices and disclosures that may be required for certain benefits, or when an employee is terminated. It is important to provide all of these legal requirements and notifications to employees, and in many cases, these must be included in an employee handbook that is given to all employees and updated regularly. These are vital procedures that protect the practice's staff, the practice itself, and of course the physician/owner.

The human resources staff of a doctor's office should monitor changes in benefits offered by the policy they offer their employees. If new limits on coverage or restrictions on which physicians are eligible for participation in the plan's approved provider network occur, it may be time to consider offering a different plan as part of the practice's benefits package. Today's employees no longer evaluate the quality of their health insurance plans based on their monthly out-of-pocket share of premiums alone.

COMPLIANCE GUIDE

Regardless of the benefits a small business offers to its employees (and, by extension, the owners—with some exceptions noted in this and future chapters of the book), there are a myriad of government rules and regulations to consider in setting up these benefits and updating them as these regulations change over time. The following chart is a helpful overview of some of the most popular employee benefits, and resources for reviewing the regulatory requirements associated with each of them. Note that laws may vary from state to state, and every small business needs to seek advice from a qualified tax advisor and an employee benefits expert to determine what it must do to comply with specific local requirements.

BENEFITS COMPLIANCE GUIDE

Item	Focus Area	Resources
Health Care Reform Employer Penalties	Businesses with 100+ full-time equivalent employees must begin providing minimum essential health insurance coverage at an affordable rate to 70% of their full-time employees in 2015 to avoid employer mandate penalties. Businesses with 50 to 99 full-time equivalent employees enjoy an additional year to comply with the employer mandate (2016 calendar year) as long as certain requirements are met. In 2016 and beyond, all businesses with 50 or more full-time equivalent employees must provide minimum essential health care coverage at an affordable rate to at least 95% of their full-time employees.	For additional information, watch the "Health Care Reform: Employer Mandate" On Demand Training under the "Training and Education" tab in the HR Support Center. Also, see the "Navigating the Employer Mandate" Guide.
Consolidated Omnibus Budget Reconciliation Act (COBRA)	COBRA applies to employers with 20 or more employees on the payroll for more than 50% of the typical business days during the previous calendar year. Some notice/disclosure requirements under COBRA include: • Initial/General COBRA Notice • COBRA Election Notice (Must include new Marketplace language) • Notice of Early Termination of COBRA • Notice of Insufficient Payment • Premium Change Notice	Sample templates are available in the "HR Forms" section under the "Essentials" tab here in the HR Support Center. Speak with your broker or COBRA administrator (if applicable) for further information about these important notice requirements.
Summary of Benefits and Coverage (SBC)	Provide a Summary of Benefits and Coverage (SBC) to inform employees regarding plan provisions. The effective date of this requirement will be determined by the reason for distribution. For participants and beneficiaries who enroll or re-enroll through an open enrollment period (including late enrollees and re-enrollees), the SBC must be provided beginning on the first day of the first open enrollment period. For participants and beneficiaries who enroll in coverage other than through an open enrollment period (including individuals who are newly eligible for coverage and special enrollees), the SBC must be provided beginning on the first day of the first plan year.	Obtain the SBC from your Health Insurance Carrier. The distribution of the document is the employer's responsibility.
Summary Plan Description (SPD)	A SPD must be provided periodically to plan participants. This document explains the features of an employer's defined benefit or defined contribution plan, including eligibility requirements, contribution formulas, vesting schedules, benefit	Speak with your health insurance broker for further information.

	calculations, and distribution options. The Employee Retirement Income Security Act (ERISA) requires that each participant receive a copy of the SPD within 90 days of joining the plan and every five years thereafter if changes are made to the SPD information or the plan is amended. Otherwise it simply must be furnished every 10 years.	
New Retirement Plan Fee Disclosures	Service providers with ERISA-covered retirement plans must provide detailed disclosure of fees being charged to plan sponsors and provide a summary of the fees. Sponsors of retirement plans with participant-directed investments plans are required to disclose certain plan fee and expense information directly to participants. Subsequent quarterly disclosures must be provided.	Speak with your retirement plan provider for further information.
Small Business Tax Credit	Determine if your small business (fewer than 25 full-time equivalent employees) qualifies for a tax credit.	Discuss this potential tax credit with your accounting professional/CPA.
Grandfathered Status Statement	Determine if your plan would be considered grandfathered (in existence with no material changes as of March 23, 2010) and perform a cost-benefit analysis of Grandfathered vs. Non-Grandfathered status.	Discuss this requirement with your health insurance broker.
Pre-existing Conditions Exclusions	Plans may no longer impose pre-existing conditions exclusions for participants.	Speak with your health insurance carrier for more information.
Evaluate FSA and/or HSA plan documents	In 2014, Section 125 Medical Reimbursement / Flexible Spending Account (FSA) plans have a maximum benefit of $2,500. This maximum will be indexed each year for inflation. Also, for flexible spending accounts, the employer gets to elect whether it would prefer to allow a carryover of $500 into the following plan year OR allow the use of a 2.5 month grace period.	Speak with your FSA plan provider for more information about these limits.
Prepare for new Form W-2 reporting requirements	Employers are responsible for reporting the total cost of medical benefits provided on each employee's Form W-2. Small employers (those that file fewer than 250 W-2 Forms in the previous tax year) are exempt until further guidance is provided.	Consult the preparer of your W-2s (payroll provider, accounting professional).
Automatic Enrollment for Employers with 200 or More Employees	Prepare to auto-enroll all new full-time employees into the health plan once they have satisfied the plan's eligibility requirements. (This requirement has been indefinitely delayed.)	See section 18A of the Fair Labor Standards Act (FLSA).
Employee	ERISA applies to employee welfare benefit plans, including	Speak with your

Retirement Income Security Act (ERISA)	group health plans, unless specifically exempted. Church and government plans are not subject to ERISA. There is not an exception for small employers. • SPD – Plan administrator must automatically provide an SPD to participants within 90 days of becoming covered by the plan and periodically thereafter. • Summary of Material Modifications (SMM) – Plan administrator must provide an SMM automatically to participants within 210 days after the end of the plan year in which the change was adopted. • Plan Documents – Plan administrator must provide copies of plan documents no later than 30 days after a written request. • Form 5500 Requirements - Form 5500 requirement applies to plan administrators of ERISA plans, unless an exception applies. Small health plans (those with fewer than 100 participants) that are fully insured, unfunded, or a combination of fully insured and unfunded, are exempt from the Form 5500 filing requirement. Summary Annual Report (SAR) - Plan administrators of ERISA plans are subject to the SAR requirement, unless an exception applies. Plans that are exempt from the annual Form 5500 filing requirement are not required to provide the SAR.	health insurance broker and health insurance carrier for more information.
Family and Medical Leave Act (FMLA)	FMLA applies to private sector employers with 50 or more employees in 20 or more workweeks in the current or preceding calendar year, as well as all public agencies and all public and private elementary and secondary schools Notice/disclosure requirements under FMLA requirements include but is not limited to: • General Notice • Certification Form • GINA Notice • Eligibility/Rights and Responsibilities Notice • Designation Notice	For a law summary, click on "Family and Medical Leave Act" in the Federal Laws section of the "Laws" tab in the HR Support Center. Each of these FMLA forms is available in the "HR Forms" section under the "Essentials" tab in the HR Support Center.
Genetic Information Nondiscrimination Act (GINA)	GINA is a federal law that prohibits discrimination in health coverage and employment based on genetic information. GINA applies to group health plans and health insurance issuers. There is not an exception for small employers.	The GINA notice can be downloaded in the "HR Forms" section under the "Essentials" tab here in the HR Support Center.
Health Insurance	HIPAA portability rules apply to group health plans and health	These forms are

Portability and Accountability Act (HIPAA)	insurance issuers, unless an exemption applies. Plans with fewer than two (2) participants who are current employees are exempt. There is no other exception for small employers. Notice/disclosure requirements HIPAA include: • Certificate of Creditable Coverage • General Notice of Preexisting Condition Exclusions • Individual Notice of Period of Preexisting Condition Exclusion • Notice of Special Enrollment Rights • Notice of Privacy Practices • Notice of Breach of Unsecured PHI (filed with U.S. Department of Health & Human Services online)	typically distributed by your health insurance carrier. Speak with your health insurance carrier if you have any questions regarding these notices.
The Children's Health Insurance Program Reauthorization Act (CHIPRA)	CHIPRA became effective April 1, 2009, creating two new special enrollment rights for employees and dependents under employer-sponsored group health plans. CHIRPA enrollment opportunities are required to be offered when an employee or eligible dependent is covered under a Medicaid plan or state children's health insurance program (CHIP), and loses eligibility under that plan; or when they become eligible under a CHIP or Medicaid plan for premium assistance that could be used toward the cost of an employer plan. There is not an exception for small employers. Employers should ensure the CHIP Notice is available.	The CHIP notice is available for download in the "HR Forms" section under the "Essentials" tab here in the HR Support Center.
Medicare Part D	Medicare Part D requirements apply to group health plan sponsors that provide prescription drug coverage to individuals who are eligible for Medicare Part D coverage. There is not an exception for small employers.	The Medicare Part D notice is available for download in the "HR Forms" section under the "Essentials" tab here in the HR Support Center.
Mental Health Parity and Addiction Equity Act (MHPAEA)	MHPAEA is a federal law that generally prevents group health plans and health insurance issuers that provide mental health and substance use disorder (MH/SUD) benefits from imposing less favorable benefit limitations on those benefits than on medical/surgical coverage. There is an exception for health plans that can demonstrate a certain cost increase and an exception for small health plans with fewer than two participants who are current employees. There is also an exception for employers with 50 or fewer employees during the preceding calendar year.	Speak with your health insurance carrier for additional details regarding this requirement.
Newborns' and Mothers' Health	NMHPA is a federal law that affects the length of time a mother and newborn child are covered for a hospital stay in connection	Speak with your health insurance

Protection Act (NMHPA)	with childbirth. NMHPA applies to group health plans that provide maternity or newborn infant coverage. There is not an exception for small employers. The plan's SPD must include a statement describing the NMHPA's protections for mothers and newborns.	carrier for additional details regarding this requirement.
Women's Health and Cancer Rights Act (WHCRA)	WHCRA helps protect many women with breast cancer who choose to have their breast reconstructed after a mastectomy The law applies to group health plans that provide coverage for mastectomy benefits. Plans with fewer than two (2) participants who are current employees (e.g., retiree health plans) are exempt. There is not an exception for small employers. Plans must provide a notice describing rights under WHCRA upon enrollment and on an annual basis after enrollment.	Speak with your health insurance carrier for additional details regarding this requirement.

*These charts are based on the law as of the publishing of this book,

but may be subject to change over time.

PART FOUR
INDIVIDUAL FINANCIAL PLANNING

Chapter 9

RISK MANAGEMENT–
PERSONAL INSURANCE BASICS

BUSINESS OWNERS SHARE many financial planning goals with individuals; to be sure, they must be vigilant to protect the assets and income streams on which they and their families depend. Therefore, planning for one's financial future as a small business owner doesn't mean "swapping" the financial planning recommendations from Part Three of this book for those included here in Part Four.

Part Four of our book looks at physicians' financial planning from an *individual* perspective. The content of all three chapters, including this one's look at personal insurance coverage, Chapter 10's overview of investments and cash, and Chapter 11, which is about retirement planning, apply to nearly every physician, regardless of how he or she earns income. The individual financial planning considerations in Part Four also apply to every physician with regard to the impact of health care reform, since we will explore how this may affect physicians and their families as *con-*

120

sumers of health care. This chapter's look at personal insurance protection needs includes medical insurance, disability insurance, life insurance, home/auto/umbrella insurance, and long-term care and critical illness protection. They are all needs that physicians share with many other Americans, particularly those with high levels of income and wealth.

MEDICAL INSURANCE

One of the most basic elements of anyone's personal financial planning is the risk coverage provided by medical insurance. People without medical insurance, or with inadequate or incomplete coverage, have been driven into bankruptcy by the high costs of medical care following a sudden injury or illness. Government programs such as Medicare and Medicaid were created in the 1960s to help the most vulnerable people in American society—the elderly and the poor. Most of the rest of us have to obtain this coverage by purchasing it from large insurance companies, either directly by individuals and families on their own, or through coverage offered as an employee benefit by companies for which we work. The recently-passed ACA (Affordable Care Act of 2010, or "health reform," or "Obamacare") requires all of us to have some form of medical insurance, although in all honesty the risks of not having coverage—bankruptcy or denial of care for conditions that threaten our health or lives—are probably worse than any penalties this new law imposes for lack of coverage.

Many medical insurance plans have changed with the passage of the ACA; in a number of cases, coverage we once considered "standard" has been subdivided into a number of different tiered plans, offering premiums that are higher or lower depending on deductibles for services such as office visits, prescription drug coverage, and hospitalization. High-wealth individuals may choose lower premiums in return for the risk of high out-of-pocket costs for prescription drugs or hospital care, but people with lower incomes may face serious financial hardship with these same plans if the care they or their family members need requires the high maximum out-of-pocket expenses mandated by some low-premium plans.

Ironically, while the number of tiered plans offered by private insurance companies and government agencies through new state and federal exchanges has increased, other options for care have become more limited with passage of the ACA. For example, there are fewer Health Maintenance Organization (HMO) plans available to consumers who wish to purchase individual and family plans, although some group plans still retain features many will recognize as HMO-type coverage; most ACA-compliant plans are structured as either Preferred Provider Organization (PPOs) or Exclusive Provider Organization (EPOs). These forms of coverage may restrict access to many consumers by being limited to individuals and families with coverage by "approved" insurance companies and government agencies. Further restrictions on care—or more accurately, reimbursement for care—may occur when PPOs and EPOs deny coverage or reduce benefits paid for services if a policy holder goes outside of the organization's network for care, or if the policy holder arranges for care without first requesting approval from the insurance provider.

While each state exchange—or the federal exchange, in states without their own—may offer different levels of coverage, the attached chart from Covered California, the official state health insurance exchange, along with additional materials from the US Department of Labor and UC Berkeley's Labor Center that provide information about subsidies for lower-income individuals, give readers insights into the complex choices many of us will face in today's health insurance marketplace.

COVERED CALIFORNIA

2014 Sliding Scale Benefits | SINGLE PERSON

Silver Plan (Eligible for Federal Subsidy)

Annual Income	$15,856 – $17,235	$17,235 – $22,980	$22,980 – $28,725	$28,725 – $45,960
Consumer Portion of Monthly Premium for Silver Plans (Balance paid by Federal subsidy)	$19 – $57	$57 – $121	$121 – $193	$193 – $364
	Copays in the Yellow Sections are Not Subject to ANY Deductible and Count Toward the Annual Out-of-Pocket Maximum		Benefits in Blue are Subject to Either a Medical Deductible, Drug Deductible or Both	
Deductible (if any)	No Deductible	$500	$1,500 Medical Deductible	$2,000 Medical Deductible
Preventative Care Copay	No Cost	No Cost	No Cost	No Cost – 1 Annual Visit
Primary Care Visit Copay	$3	$15	$40	$45
Specialty Care Visit Copay	$5	$20	$50	$65
Urgent Care Visit Copay	$6	$30	$80	$90
Lab Testing Copay	$3	$15	$40	$45
X-Ray Copay	$5	$20	$50	$65
Generic Medication Copay	$3	$5	$20	$25
Emergency Room Copay	$25	$75	$250	$250
High cost and infrequent services like Hospital Care and Outpatient Surgery	10%	15%	20% of your plan's negotiated rate	20% of your plan's negotiated rate
Brand medications may be subject to Annual Drug Deductible before you pay the Copay	No Deductible	$50 then pay the copay amount	$250 then pay the copay amount	$250 then pay the copay amount
Preferred brand Copay after Drug Deductible	$5	$15	$30	$50
MAXIMUM OUT-OF-POCKET FOR ONE	$2,250	$2,250	$5,200	$6,350
MAXIMUM OUT-OF-POCKET FOR FAMILY	$4,500	$4,500	$10,400	$12,700

New Health Insurance Marketplace Coverage Options and Your Health Coverage

Form Approved
OMB No. 1210-0149
(expires 11-30-2013)

PART A: General Information

When key parts of the health care law take effect in 2014, there will be a new way to buy health insurance: the Health Insurance Marketplace. To assist you as you evaluate options for you and your family, this notice provides some basic information about the new Marketplace and employment-based health coverage offered by your employer.

What is the Health Insurance Marketplace?

The Marketplace is designed to help you find health insurance that meets your needs and fits your budget. The Marketplace offers "one-stop shopping" to find and compare private health insurance options. You may also be eligible for a new kind of tax credit that lowers your monthly premium right away. Open enrollment for health insurance coverage through the Marketplace begins in October 2013 for coverage starting as early as January 1, 2014.

Can I Save Money on my Health Insurance Premiums in the Marketplace?

You may qualify to save money and lower your monthly premium, but only if your employer does not offer coverage, or offers coverage that doesn't meet certain standards. The savings on your premium that you're eligible for depends on your household income.

Does Employer Health Coverage Affect Eligibility for Premium Savings through the Marketplace?

Yes. If you have an offer of health coverage from your employer that meets certain standards, you will not be eligible for a tax credit through the Marketplace and may wish to enroll in your employer's health plan. However, you may be eligible for a tax credit that lowers your monthly premium, or a reduction in certain cost-sharing if your employer does not offer coverage to you at all or does not offer coverage that meets certain standards. If the cost of a plan from your employer that would cover you (and not any other members of your family) is more than 9.5% of your household income for the year, or if the coverage your employer provides does not meet the "minimum value" standard set by the Affordable Care Act, you may be eligible for a tax credit.[1]

Note: If you purchase a health plan through the Marketplace instead of accepting health coverage offered by your employer, then you may lose the employer contribution (if any) to the employer-offered coverage. Also, this employer contribution -as well as your employee contribution to employer-offered coverage- is often excluded from income for Federal and State income tax purposes. Your payments for coverage through the Marketplace are made on an after-tax basis.

How Can I Get More Information?

For more information about your coverage offered by your employer, please check your summary plan description or contact _____ .

The Marketplace can help you evaluate your coverage options, including your eligibility for coverage through the Marketplace and its cost. Please visit HealthCare.gov for more information, including an online application for health insurance coverage and contact information for a Health Insurance Marketplace in your area.

---

[1] An employer-sponsored health plan meets the "minimum value standard" if the plan's share of the total allowed benefit costs covered by the plan is no less than 60 percent of such costs.

PART B: Information About Health Coverage Offered by Your Employer

This section contains information about any health coverage offered by your employer. If you decide to complete an application for coverage in the Marketplace, you will be asked to provide this information. This information is numbered to correspond to the Marketplace application.

3. Employer name	4. Employer Identification Number (EIN)
5. Employer address	6. Employer phone number
7. City	8. State / 9. ZIP code

10. Who can we contact about employee health coverage at this job?	
11. Phone number (if different from above)	12. Email address

Here is some basic information about health coverage offered by this employer:

- As your employer, we offer a health plan to:
  - ☐ All employees.

  - ☐ Some employees. Eligible employees are:

- With respect to dependents:
  - ☐ We do offer coverage. Eligible dependents are:

  - ☐ We do not offer coverage.

☐ If checked, this coverage meets the minimum value standard, and the cost of this coverage to you is intended to be affordable, based on employee wages.

∗∗ Even if your employer intends your coverage to be affordable, you may still be eligible for a premium discount through the Marketplace. The Marketplace will use your household income, along with other factors, to determine whether you may be eligible for a premium discount. If, for example, your wages vary from week to week (perhaps you are an hourly employee or you work on a commission basis), if you are newly employed mid-year, or if you have other income losses, you may still qualify for a premium discount.

If you decide to shop for coverage in the Marketplace, HealthCare.gov will guide you through the process. Here's the employer information you'll enter when you visit HealthCare.gov to find out if you can get a tax credit to lower your monthly premiums.

The information below corresponds to the Marketplace Employer Coverage Tool. Completing this section is optional for employers, but will help ensure employees understand their coverage choices.

13. **Is the employee currently eligible for coverage offered by this employer, or will the employee be eligible in the next 3 months?**

☐ **Yes** (Continue)

   13a. If the employee is not eligible today, including as a result of a waiting or probationary period, when is the

   employee eligible for coverage? _____ (mm/dd/yyyy) (Continue)

☐ **No** (STOP and return this form to employee)

14. Does the employer offer a health plan that meets the minimum value standard*?
    ☐ Yes (Go to question 15) ☐ No (STOP and return form to employee)

15. For the lowest-cost plan that meets the minimum value standard* offered **only to the employee** (don't include family plans): If the employer has wellness programs, provide the premium that the employee would pay if he/ she received the maximum discount for any tobacco cessation programs, and didn't receive any other discounts based on wellness programs.
    a. How much would the employee have to pay in premiums for this plan? $
    b. How often? ☐ Weekly ☐ Every 2 weeks ☐ Twice a month ☐ Monthly ☐ Quarterly ☐ Yearly

If the plan year will end soon and you know that the health plans offered will change, go to question 16. If you don't know, STOP and return form to employee.

16. What change will the employer make for the new plan year?
    ☐ Employer won't offer health coverage
    ☐ Employer will start offering health coverage to employees or change the premium for the lowest-cost plan available only to the employee that meets the minimum value standard.* (Premium should reflect the discount for wellness programs. See question 15.)
    a. How much will the employee have to pay in premiums for that plan? $
    b. How often? ☐ Weekly ☐ Every 2 weeks ☐ Twice a month ☐ Monthly ☐ Quarterly ☐ Yearly

    Date of change (mm/dd/yyyy):

• An employer-sponsored health plan meets the "minimum value standard" if the plan's share of the total allowed benefit costs covered by the plan is no less than 60 percent of such costs (Section 36B(c)(2)(C)(ii) of the Internal Revenue Code of 1986)

UC BERKELEY
LABOR
CENTER

Modified Adjusted Gross Income under the Affordable Care Act
November 2013

Under the Affordable Care Act, eligibility for income-based Medicaid[1] and subsidized health insurance through the Exchanges will be calculated using a household's Modified Adjusted Gross Income (MAGI). The Affordable Care Act definition of MAGI under the Internal Revenue Code[2] and federal Medicaid regulations[3] is shown below. For most individuals who will apply for health coverage under the Affordable Care Act, MAGI will be equal to Adjusted Gross Income. This document summarizes relevant federal regulations; it is not personalized tax or legal advice. Consult the Health Insurance Marketplace for your state, your local Medicaid agency, or a legal or tax advisor for assistance in determining your MAGI.

Modified Adjusted Gross Income (MAGI) =

Adjusted Gross Income (AGI)

Line 4 on a Form 1040EZ

Line 21 on a Form 1040A

Line 37 on a Form 1040

Include:
- Wages, salaries, tips, etc.
- Taxable interest
- Taxable amount of pension, annuity or IRA distributions and Social Security benefits[4]
- Business income, farm income, capital gain, other gains (or loss)
- Unemployment compensation
- Ordinary dividends
- Alimony received
- Rental real estate, royalties, partnerships, S corporations, trusts, etc.
- Taxable refunds, credits, or offsets of state and local income taxes
- Other income

Deduct:
- Certain self-employed expenses[5]
- Student loan interest deduction
- Educator expenses
- IRA deduction
- Moving expenses
- Penalty on early withdrawal of savings
- Health savings account deduction
- Alimony paid
- Domestic production activities deduction
- Certain business expenses of reservists, performing artists, and fee-basis government officials

Note: Check the IRS website for detailed requirements for the income and deduction categories above. Do not include Veterans' disability payments, workers' compensation or child support received. Pre-tax contributions, such as those for child care, commuting, employer-sponsored health insurance, flexible spending accounts and retirement plans such as 401(k) and 403(b), are not included in AGI but are not listed above because they are already subtracted out of W-2 wages and salaries.

+ Add back certain income
- Non-taxable Social Security benefits[4] (Line 20a minus 20b on a Form 1040)
- Tax-exempt interest (Line on 8b on a Form 1040)
- Foreign earned income & housing expenses for Americans living abroad (calculated on a Form 2555)

For Medicaid eligibility
− Exclude from income
- Scholarships, awards, or fellowship grants used for education purposes and not for living expenses
- Certain American Indian and Alaska Native income derived from distributions, payments, ownership interests, real property usage rights, and student financial assistance
- An amount received as a lump sum is counted as income only in the month received

[1] Medicaid eligibility is generally based on MAGI for parents and childless adults under age 65, children and pregnant women, but not for individuals eligible on the basis of being aged, blind, or disabled.
[2] Internal Revenue Code Section 36B(d)(2)(B)
[3] Public Health and Welfare Code Section 435.603(e)
[4] "Social Security benefits" includes disability payments (SSDI), but does not include Supplemental Security Income (SSI), which should be excluded.
[5] Deductible part of self-employment tax; SEP, SIMPLE, and qualified plans; health insurance deduction

These charts reference the income limits the government uses to determine who receives or should receive a subsidy for medical insurance coverage, and at what percent of the total costs these subsidies are to be offered. They also describe who should be covered by Medicaid (in this case, the state of California's Medi-Cal program) and receive free health care. In general terms, the government looks at the number of people in a household and at the total income for the household in setting these eligibility requirements for subsidies or free care. Total income includes many sources, both earned and unearned, to determine these eligibilities. While they are based on specific dollar amounts of income (adjusted for family size), levels of subsidy coverage are expressed in terms of a "poverty level," or an estimated household income that is used to define eligibility for a broad range of government assistance programs. There are different levels above this poverty level, expressed as multiples of it; individuals or families with income levels of two or three times the poverty level are eligible for different and usually lower subsidies than those at the poverty level itself. If income falls to a level at or below the poverty level threshold, then the individual or the family will qualify for Medicaid (Medi-Cal) and receive free care independent of the subsidies offered for policies purchased through the state exchange. However, the family can choose to pay 100% of the premium if they do not wish to be on Medi-Cal. However, this freedom of choice may be moot given the inability of people at the poverty level to afford the full cost of medical insurance.

These financial calculations are very difficult to understand, and yet they affect levels of expense—and income—in the medical field more than they affect any other businesses in the United States. The business offices of medical practices require highly skilled and trained staff to provide information to the human resource department in terms of benefits offered.

But more important, they must know these regulations in order to assist members of the public who come to the practice for care, and how much they can count on government programs to provide financial assistance when it is required. This information is also vital to the physician's business office, since revenue from government programs is most if not all of the income to be earned by providing care that meets the needs of many of their patients and community members.

DISABILITY INSURANCE

Another important element of sound financial planning for an individual or family is disability income insurance. As described above in Part Three of this book, many companies offer long-term disability insurance as part of their employee benefit packages. Yet most people don't understand the importance of considering their own need for disability insurance beyond the sometimes-limited coverage included by employer-provided policies.

Concerns for the physician as an individual covered by disability insurance begin with the same concerns they may have as small business owners. As mentioned in previous chapters of this book, they will likely need to purchase disability coverage with higher monthly payments to take care of business expenses, and will need to consider this and other types of insurance to protect the business's operations if the physician (or any of the other practice owners) will be unable to work for a lengthy period of time. And speaking of time, a second variable in disability insurance is also worth mentioning: the length of time between the filing of a claim and the initiation of monthly payments. Whether a physician is covered by a group or individual plan, it is important to verify the time at which benefits will begin. Group plans can have a short waiting period—even zero days—while costs of covering a group of employees are still reasonable. Individual plans usually have a ninety-day waiting period and premiums may be higher. But coverage by individual plans is also more flexible and can be designed to be more comprehensive.

But these concerns are covered earlier in the book. In this section, we want to be sure to remind readers that they need to have coverage that protects themselves and their families from a long-term interruption in revenue. Saving the business is one thing, but no financial plan is complete without a risk management strategy that takes into account the monthly or annual income requirements of the physician outside of the workplace. Estimating these expenses, including mortgage/rent for the family home, automobile payments, and all the other items one would include in a family budget, is something we make sure is covered in our work with all of our small business clients. It's not a topic that is normally overlooked; in fact, many individuals start with their family's financial needs when they begin the risk management portion of their financial plans. However, we have seen physicians get distracted by the complexities of all the insurance products they need to consider when dealing with the professional side of their plan.

The real risk in dealing with these complexities is to make sure the total financial responsibilities of a physician are covered by insurance and other risk management strategies. When it comes to disability insurance, the reality is that most policies reach an upper limit on the amount of coverage anyone may buy. In many cases, these upper limits aren't sufficient to meet the monthly financial needs of a physician, particularly when all the needs for covering business expenses and personal financial obligations are added together. As noted below, there are strategies for handling these monthly requirements for disability coverage, even if the solutions aren't traditional "disability" insurance products. But while we're discussing the individual aspects of a physician's disability coverage, we will also raise a non-insurance policy and perhaps a non-risk management aspect of our recommendations for making sure a physician's individual needs are included in his or her plan. And that is the "behavioral" aspect of individual vs. business financial planning.

In some cases, the monthly limits for disability coverage will require the assembly of a complicated plan to meet potential monthly expenses that exceed the limits of any single policy's coverage. In the case of a multi-owner physicians' practice, it may be no simple task to assemble enough coverage for each owner to guarantee the business will survive should any one of them become disabled. This may make the second but equally important reason for disability coverage—ensuring the financial security of each physician's family in the event of disability—a difficult subject to raise. There are two reasons for this: first, if the partners believe it is a "stretch" to assemble a complex risk management strategy for the practice, or if the premiums and/or cash reserves needed for business continuity are high, they may not be as willing to address their needs for additional complexities and premiums for even more disability insurance, even if it is absolutely necessary to do so. Second, the partners may come to the awkward realization that each of them has very different personal financial obligations that need to be covered, so that the amount of their disability coverage will not be the same for every partner. One partner may have children in college, while another is young and single. Sometimes a partner may enjoy the finer things in life, while his or her colleague may live a less extravagant lifestyle. Issues of equity might arise in these cases, and will need to be faced and addressed.

The partners may agree to cover everyone's personal financial obligations regardless of the amount involved, or they may not. There is no universal right or wrong answer, of course, as is the case with so many other elements of a good financial plan. But it would be irresponsible for the partners not to address this issue, since one consequence might be the decision to move away from uncomfortable discussions and leave out this important detail in each partner's financial plan. Situations like these are opportunities for financial planners to provide services that are an integral part of our work, even if they seem more like counseling than elements of a "pure" financial plan. They are yet another reason for us to remind readers about the benefits of engaging the services of a professional financial planner.

We generally approach our conversations with clients in a matter-of-fact way, beginning with the basics of how disability insurance works, and even how "disability" is defined. In general terms disability can be caused by a variety of different factors. Changes in health status, accidents, sickness, or any other circumstance that causes one not to be able to continue working in their own occupation, or even any occupation, are the primary reasons for disability insurance. It is designed to replace the income that would be lost in these cases. The question that one needs to ask himself or herself is, "What if I become disabled? Would I lose most or all of my income?" If the answer is yes, then having disability insurance to replace that income is essential. This way you can have cash flow coming in to help pay for mortgage payments, food, and other bare necessities. Most disability policies cover 60 to 70% of a person's net income up to a maximum of between $15,000 and $20,000 per month. In some cases these amounts may not be enough to provide enough cash flow for a physician accustomed to monthly income beyond these levels. Luckily, there is an alternative option for physicians or any business owners in this situation.

Because many physicians' monthly income requirements plus their share of their office's overhead expenses exceed the $15,000 to $20,000 monthly limits on disability insurance, policies called business overhead expense insurance are worth consideration. The additional income they provide may be the difference between maintaining the physician's family's lifestyle and continued participation in his or her practice, or failing to meet both of these obligations. One additional benefit of this type of coverage is that premiums for business overhead expense policies may be tax-deductible. The importance of having an adequate amount of cash flow in the event of a physician's disability can be essential to the continued functioning of the practice while a physician is out on disability. In addition to meeting regular monthly overhead costs without the income a disabled physician would contribute, there may be a need for additional staff or maybe even another physician to step in and take over for a while until everything is back to normal again.

For those physicians who do have multiple partners in the business, it is extremely important to consider disability insurance as a tool for business continuation planning in the event of a prolonged absence. In these cases, buy/sell agreements need to be funded and coordinated with disability insurance as described earlier in Chapter 8. Consideration of these risk management strategies is equally important for the physician as an individual as they are for the business itself; without adequate plans to protect income streams during a time when the physician cannot earn fees to contribute to the business, risks to everyone, including the physician and his or her family, may become unmanageable. There may be no practice to return to after a prolonged disability is over and personal expenses beyond the maximum provided by standard individual disability insurance are not met for months on end or more.

These risks are often poorly understood. People simply don't believe they need to plan for maintaining an income stream should they become disabled due to accident or illness; many individuals believe that significant risks for becoming disabled only apply to people of retirement age. But the fact is that, in America today, there are nearly 20 million people between the ages of twenty-one and sixty-four who are disabled—50% of the total number of disabled people in the United States. The Social Security Administration estimates that one out of every four twenty-year-old Americans will become disabled before reaching the age of sixty-seven.[1]

Disability income insurance isn't cheap, and its cost can be a deterrent for many who need it. Because it isn't always considered as fully as life insurance coverage or retirement savings, the risks of either ignoring the need for coverage completely, or purchasing a plan that either provides inadequate income replacement or costs more than it should, are excellent reasons for consulting a qualified insurance consultant about the potential benefits of including disability insurance in a physician's financial plan.

Although policies are still available in the commercial insurance marketplace, adequate disability insurance is becoming more difficult to obtain as definitions of disability and limits on years of coverage vary. Some policies that were sold many years ago have a very rich and extended definition of the disabilit(ies) that qualify for payment of benefits; many newer policies define disability in more narrow and specific terms. Some policies pay a lifetime benefit in the event of disability, but most policies today cover up to age sixty-five or sixty-seven. The definition of disability and other policy features are extremely important. It is not the cost of coverage that matters as much as how the policy will pay if someone becomes

---

1 http://www.disabilitycanhappen.org/chances_disability/disability_stats.asp and http://www.ssa.gov/planners/disability/

disabled. Another key consideration is whether or not the policy is considered "non-cancelable and guaranteed renewable" or just "non-cancelable." Both are important features to have in any disability insurance policy, but they are better in combination. In the first case, the policy owner has the right to continue the policy, and the insurance company can neither change the benefits and features of the policy nor its premiums. In the latter case, the policy is also guaranteed to continue in force as long as premiums are paid, and its benefits and features cannot be changed. However, the premium for a "noncancelable" policy can be increased for an entire class of policy holders by the insurance carrier, with appropriate state government approval. In both cases, policies are normally guaranteed to remain in place through age sixty-five. Even so, the definition of disability that qualifies for payment of benefits is still a key element of any such policy, because this describes the circumstances under which the policy will pay benefits, and, in some cases, how they will pay them.

While on the subject of disability insurance, we also recommend that physicians and other individual clients understand what is covered under Social Security, and how Social Security pays in the event of short term or long-term disability. Most people do not understand these benefits and how little Social Security actually pays in these circumstances, or the definition of disability Social Security uses to determine eligibility. The following description of these benefits, as they are described on the Social Security Administration's website, illustrate the strict (and restrictive) rules used to define disability, and the lengthy time (one year) before any benefits are paid:

"The definition of disability under Social Security is different than other programs. Social Security pays only for total disability. **No benefits are payable for partial disability or for short-term disability**.

"'Disability' under Social Security is based on your inability to work. We consider you disabled under Social Security rules if:

"You cannot do work that you did before;

"We decide that you cannot adjust to other work because of your medical condition(s); **and**

"Your disability has lasted or is expected to last for at least one year or to result in death.

"This is a strict definition of disability. Social Security program rules assume that working families have access to other resources to provide support during periods of short-term disabilities, including workers' compensation, insurance, savings and investments."[2]

Note also that there are two different ways in which the Social Security Administration pays disability claims. "Regular" Social Security Disability Insurance, described above, pays benefits for workers who have established eligibility by paying a qualifying amount of Social Security Taxes. "Supplemental Security Income" (SSI) is a benefit paid to Americans who are aged, blind, and/or disabled and have little or no income. Its payments are designed to pay for basics such as food, clothing and shelter. Unlike Social Security Disability Insurance, SSI payments are provided to individuals in need regardless of whether they have paid Social Security Taxes. In general terms, it is a lot more difficult to qualify for Social Security benefits in the event of disability, as their coverage is limited to situations we would define as severe. We recommend private disability insurance plans offered through insurance carriers, whose policies use a broader definition of disability; in fact, as shown in the above-quoted description of these benefits from the Social Security Administration, they share in this opinion. Specifically, private carriers are more likely to pay

2 http://www.ssa.gov/disability/

claims for the inability to perform the policy holder's "own occupation," which covers the person's occupation at the time of loss.

LIFE INSURANCE

Everyone knows life insurance is important; however, there are many misconceptions about it, and mistakes people often make because they don't understand how to include life insurance in their personal financial plan.

First, life insurance can be used as a financial tool to protect against issues such as paying off a loan/debt such as a mortgage, student loans, business loans, income replacement for a family member or loved ones, college funding needs for children, business income needs, buy/sell agreement funding for a business, or estate planning to provide liquidity for paying taxes and other costs. Most people/physicians don't have the proper or adequate amount of insurance. Today life insurance is a way more versatile tool for insurance and other financial planning needs. Time with a professional financial planner and life insurance expert may be required to fully understand the different policies that are available, and how they need to be designed in order to provide maximum coverage for a practicing physician.

There are also several different types of life insurance, each of which meets its own set of unique and limited needs. There is Term Life, which usually provides coverage in "terms" that can be ten, twenty, or thirty years long. Term life policies typically expire and cease providing coverage at the end of these terms, with no residual cash value returned to the policy owner if he or she outlives the term of the policy. Term life policies are pure cost insurance and don't offer any other advantages. Universal Life is a more "permanent" solution, because the client can actually arrange the policy to last as long as he or she wishes, and as long as premiums are paid, the policy can last for as long as a person is alive. Unlike term insurance, the policy does not expire automatically, but only expires in the event there isn't enough cash available to sustain the policy's coverage obligations.

Life insurance policies may or may not have guarantees, and one must pay very close attention to determine what guarantees are being offered with these policies. What the guarantees mean is that the insurance company provides a guaranteed payment of the policy's death benefit as long as the insured meets the policy's requirements and conditions, chief among them the payment of certain levels of premiums. These guarantees may be set to expire at an agreed-on age, or they may be for life. Guaranteed policies may also include the option for the insured to continue the insurance at a given age, with premiums to be determined, based on the needs of the insured. Naturally, policy holders should be sure there are written guarantees in the policy, and they should also be confident in the reliability and reputation of the insurance carrier. These and other considerations may need to be properly explained by the insurance professional.

Factors to consider in purchasing insurance include interest rates at which coverage may be increased to adjust for inflation, and premium payment requirements that may be necessary to receive a specific death benefit guarantee. There are also Variable Life policies, which may be more risky, and may or may not have certain guarantees in place. Variable life policy holders may be accepting more risk by agreeing that a portion of their policy's value would be invested in "subaccounts" that resembled mutual stock funds; policy holders can select from a range of subaccounts that are offered in the plan. These variable policies were extremely popular during the 1980s through the early 2000s due to the increases in the value of the stock market. Variable life policies required the insured to choose how the cash portion of their policies would be invested, essentially offering them the benefits of increasing stock market values, but also putting them at risk of losing value in times when the stock market went down (hence the times during which these policies were most popular). Most of these policies do not provide long-lasting guarantees, which means that the cash portion of the policy is not guaranteed and can fluctuate based on the performance of the underlying subaccounts. As a result, a person may lose some or all of the policy's death benefit, or the policy may be canceled in its entirety if there is not value in the policy to sustain its future obligations. These sorts of policies are more risky and therefore may or may not be suitable for some people. Clients are recommended to seek the advice of a financial professional to determine whether such policies are appropriate for them.

Some Whole Life policies not only offer some level of guarantees; they also may pay dividends throughout the life of the policy. These dividends, which are based on the insurance company's financial performance and may vary based on the company's decision on the amount and timing of these dividends each year, can be used to purchase more insurance, or to add to the policy's accumulating cash value. The flexibility that these whole life policies provide allows people to choose how they wish to use their policies' cash values and dividends to work in their favor. Some people prefer more death benefit, and for this reason they may request that the dividends and cash value continue to accumulate in the policy, in which case the death benefit will increase. Others may need cash at some point and they may choose to receive those dividends or cash values in a form of monthly or annual payments. In doing so the death benefit will not grow as fast, but in turn the client will receive more cash and income over the life of the policy.

It is also recommended that any changes to the policy be thoroughly reviewed with a qualified insurance consultant or professional, which would be a key step in making sure that the client is aware of all of the positives and negatives about decisions involving cash value, death benefits, guarantees, and other aspects of a whole life policy. One thing a life insurance policy does provide is a tax-favored treatment for access to cash, and for increases in these policies' cash values as compared to other investment products. These tax considerations should also be reviewed with a qualified insurance consultant.

It's very important that, when it comes to insurance, people should NOT listen to the advice of anyone who is not trained in this area and who doesn't have a thorough understanding of these products. Sometimes people listen to their friends, their CPA, or peer groups, but these may or may not be reliable sources of help; their general advice may not apply to the individual aspects of the policy holder they're trying to "help." Someone else's past experience or previous understanding of a financial product doesn't mean advice based on these experiences is appropriate for any particular policy holder. Physicians and other individuals need to do their own research, and also need to consider their own vision of what they would like their plans to do in the future, rather than listening to someone else's opinion of how their own financial future should look.

There are other, less-understood risks and opportunities to consider when including life insurance in one's financial plan. One risk is the stability of the company from which a physician purchases life insurance, regardless of the type selected. It is very important to understand the financial ratings of the insurance carrier, since the guarantees are only backed by the financial strength of the carrier. A possible opportunity may result from the unique tax treatments of certain life insurance policies. Many professionals and physicians may use life insurance cash values to accumulate savings, and be able to use these funds to supplement revenue streams as needed in future years. A risk and opportunity exists in policies that allow for loans to be taken out against accumulated cash value. The advantage is that these loans are typically offered at low reasonable interest rates; however, they also decrease the accumulating cash value of policies that offer these loans. Finally, most people forget to update the beneficiaries on their policies, which is a substantial risk. Beneficiaries must be reviewed on a regular basis to make sure all is correct. If a living trust is established, this trust itself may or may not be appropriate to add as a beneficiary; in these cases, policy holders must check with their estate planning attorneys.

While living trusts are covered in more detail later in this book, this brief overview of their purpose and key features, from the American Bar Association, is a good introduction:

"A living trust—an inter vivos trust if you want to be formal—allows you to put your assets in a trust while you're still alive. If your living trust is revocable, as almost all are, it gives you great flexibility. You or someone in whom you have confidence manages the property, usually for the benefit of you or your family. Most people name themselves as trustees, and find there is no difference between managing the trust and managing their own property—they have the right to buy, sell, or give property as before, though the property is in the trust's name rather than their own.

"A living trust is one of the two main ways to avoid probate. (The other is joint tenancy or survivorship.) One of the purposes of probate is to determine the disposition of the property you leave at death. Since the trustee of your living trust owns that property, there is no need for probate.

"Living trusts have become extremely popular in recent years. Even though they're a useful, simple, and relatively inexpensive way to plan your estate, they do not magically solve all your problems.

"For example, as states have simplified their probate procedures, many of the advantages of living trusts have diminished. And though they're great for some people, you can't assume they're great for you.

"Deciding whether a living trust is right for you depends on the size of your estate, what kinds of assets it contains, and what plans you have for yourself and your family."[3]

HOME/AUTO/UMBRELLA INSURANCE

Everyone must have these policies, but most people may not have the proper level of protection, especially physicians. An individual's or family's home and car policies must be reviewed to be sure that the coverage is adequate for liability purposes; a single accident or lawsuit must never have the potential to result in an award to a third party that exceeds the policy value and therefore may require draining of savings, loss of assets, or worse. Also, if there is a living trust, this entity should be added as named insured; this is a detail that many people miss. If they establish a living trust, most people record their home's ownership to include the name of this living trust. But if they fail to add the name of this living trust as a named insured on their homeowner insurance policy, the living trust may not be covered in the event of a lawsuit. For this reason, practically anyone who has any ownership of the property should be considered for listing as a named insured on a homeowner policy.

Purchasing an umbrella policy offers important reassurance for in-

---

3 http://www.americanbar.org/content/dam/aba/migrated/publiced/practical/books/wills/chapter_5.authcheckdam.pdf

dividuals and families, because it ensures that any liability extends to the coverage limits of both automobile and homeowner policies in the event of lawsuits or other liabilities. An umbrella policy is essential in these cases because it provides additional liability protection above and beyond the coverage that is originally included in the homeowners or the auto insurance policy. What this means is that if someone gets sued for $1 million in an auto accident and their auto policy has a $300,000 limit, without an umbrella policy, the $300,000 limit of the automobile policy is all the insurance company is obligated to pay. No matter how much homeowners insurance coverage the individual in this case has, without the protection "umbrella" coverage provides, it will not apply to the auto accident lawsuit. An umbrella policy extends coverage for a lawsuit like this to the maximum value of all policies covered under the "umbrella." This same individual with such an umbrella policy would have access to the remaining $700,000 through the linked homeowner's policy, as long as it is equal to or greater than the $700,000 required to cover the $1 million lawsuit. This is a very important asset protection strategy for physicians, who typically own many insurance policies, and who are also subject to large lawsuits from a variety of potential claimants.

ADDITIONAL COVERAGE FOR RARE EVENTS

Most homeowner's insurance policies do not include coverage for losses in floods or earthquakes. Policies to cover specific disaster-related losses should be added separately to protect against them. If a person lives near an earthquake-prone area, then it is recommended they purchase earthquake insurance to protect themselves as much as possible. If people live near a flood zone, it is required in most cases that they have flood insurance; an added benefit of this specific coverage is that it also protects against damage caused by rising water defined broadly, which includes rain. Most homeowners policies do not cover rising water which could technically be defined as a "flood," which is excluded from these policies. Our advice is to review the definitions for specific risks covered or not covered by a homeowners policy, and consult with a qualified insurance professional to see if anything needs to be remedied to provide coverage for risks that may be assumed to be included in a policy but in fact may not. These may be essential, depending on the value of one's home and liquid assets. Standard homeowner policies are notorious for excluding coverage for floods and earthquakes, and, depending on the location of a physician's property and the likelihood of damage from these risks, many doctors have shared the tragic discovery that, after such a loss, they are not covered despite purchasing what they believed was adequate insurance.

Understanding how your homeowners, auto insurance, and umbrella policies are designed is an important part of developing a complete financial plan to make sure that all assets are properly protected, and to also ensure coverage for associated legal expenses, which are normally provided under the liability portion of the policy. It is also important to make sure that any children who have reached the driving age are added to the policy to provide complete protection of the family's assets. This is another reason why umbrella policies are important, because younger people are more likely to get into accidents.

LONG-TERM CARE AND CRITICAL ILLNESS POLICIES

These polices are becoming more popular due to the health issues we face as medical science advances and new, life-extending care is possible.

However, just because people are living longer doesn't mean we are living healthier. In many cases, "end-of-life care," nursing homes, hospice care, and other similar institutionalizations are a part of life that is not only confining and emotionally difficult for individuals and their families alike; they can also be a financial disaster, draining savings, other assets, and even one's home to provide required care.

Some people have family history of cancer and other cognitive impairments and therefore may have a higher risk to these potential health issues. Long-term care policies offer financial protection against certain risks that may cause a person not to be able to perform two out of five or six activities of daily living, such as eating, bathing, dressing, toileting, and transferring. This test determines whether a person is able to perform these activities; if they cannot, they are likely to need assistance either at home or through placement into a special facility such as a nursing home or another similar facility. Since such care always costs a lot of money each month, it is essential to have long-term care insurance to pay for these costs.

Furthermore, it is important—not only for asset protection but also for retirement planning—to ensure that a long-term care policy is in effect. These policies protect cash accounts or other investments an individual or family may have, while protecting their retirement income so that no additional money would be needed to pay for such care. An example of the risk these policies help control is a person living comfortably off their retirement income until a sudden health situation develops and he or she needs an additional $3,000 per month to pay for long-term care. This may put a huge dent in the retirement plan and cause cash and investments to be depleted much more quickly than anticipated. To protect assets and income from these types of risk, one must consider purchasing a long-term care insurance policy.

While long-term care and critical illness policies can offer protection in these circumstances, costs for care are becoming so high that most insurance policies in these categories have changed a great deal over the years. There are some life insurance policies that now offer long-term care alongside life insurance, which may be a good alternative insurance planning tool. These plans have evolved and policies have become a bit more expensive compared to what one could have purchased several years ago. What's important for people to understand is that there are different kinds of policies that provide long-term care insurance. Due to the fact that most carriers have reduced the total lifetime benefit to a maximum of somewhere between five to ten years of payments, many people are seeking other types of long-term care coverage which now include plans that combine life insurance and long-term care riders to protect people who may need long-term care beyond the limits of other policies.

Disability insurance replaces one's income in the event of an accident or sickness, but long-term care pays for the cost of home care or facility. Another name for it is custodial care or skilled nursing and facility care. In some cases, these policies pay "benefits" not to the individual, but instead to the professionals providing this care.

Many government agencies are now sending letters to their citizens—particularly senior citizens—asking them to consider purchasing private long-term care insurance, since the government no longer provides long-term care insurance. Unless a person has extremely low income, and limited coverage is provided through Medicaid, long-term care insurance needs careful consideration in any financial plan.

Chapter 10

WEALTH ACCUMULATON I–
INVESTMENT CASH, AND TAX PLANNING BASICS

THIS NEXT CHAPTER OF OUR LOOK at individual financial planning presents an overview of several different types of investment options available for physicians as individuals or members of a family. It also includes a brief reminder about one of the most important considerations in any investment strategy—cash—and the introduction of several tax planning concepts that can affect the success of many investment programs. Note that this general look at investment instruments is separate from retirement planning, which is not only a subset of any individual financial plan, but is also a topic that can be better understood in light of some of the basic information about investment options presented in this chapter. In our presentation of investment strategies, we will limit our discussions to mutual funds, professionally managed accounts, and annuities. We will refrain from discussing the advantages of assembling one's own individual portfolio of individual stocks, day trading, derivatives, or other specialized investment instruments. This book is about the development and ongoing implementation of a comprehensive financial and practice management plan, and it is based on the assumption that a physician, whether he or she is an employee of a hospital or large health care organization, owns a private practice either alone or with other providers, or is a professor at an academic institution, has investment options related to one or more of these professional career options. There are other books with information on the investment options that will not be covered in this book.

MUTUAL FUNDS

Mutual funds are one of the oldest investment instruments available today. One of the earliest examples of this idea goes back to 1774 in the Netherlands, where a merchant named Abraham van Ketwich designed an investment instrument combining multiple securities, including foreign government bonds and plantation loans. Called "negotiatie" in Dutch, this fund was named "Eendragt Maakt Magt," or "Unity Creates Strength." The concept spread throughout Europe and England in the 19th Century; in fact, the Foreign and Colonial Government Trust, founded in 1868, is still traded on the London Stock Exchange today. America's first such fund was the Boston Personal Property Trust, formed in 1893. Mutual funds grew in number and diversity for the next several decades. The Alexander Fund, established in Philadelphia in 1907, was the first to allow investors to make withdrawals on demand and is therefore seen by some financial historians as the first modern mutual fund. The mutual fund industry collapsed after the stock market crash of 1929, and wasn't significantly revived until the end of World War II. Mutual funds have grown rapidly since then, sparked by the first indexed funds and money market funds in the 1970s. Today there are over 14,000 mutual funds available to investors.

Mutual funds are pools of funds, which are managed by professional money managers and their team of researchers, allowing investors to participate in American and international equities and bond investments. Diversification is one of the ways to spread the risk over multiple asset classes and to reduce the overall risk. Each fund has its own goal and investment styles and investors would need to establish a risk profile, time horizon and review their goals before investing in any financial investments and assets. The chart on the next page shows the history of funds from different sectors from 1995 through 2015 and how they may differ in performance from one year to the next.

This chart shows the performance of different asset classes over a twenty-year period, showing large cap, mid cap, and small cap stocks; bonds; and international stocks, and how they may differ in performance from year to year. The dark black line and the squares it intersects show a diversified portfolio's performance. A basic risk management strategy for all investors to employ as they create an investment program is to diversify, in order to mitigate risks that might be specific to a single market. More sophisticated investors, and investors who are either more comfortable with risk or more willing to adjust their portfolios quickly in response to changes in the nature of one or more markets, may leave this initial advice behind. In many cases, these investors consider managing their portfolios as their primary, or even full-time jobs. For the rest of us, diversification is a good way to go.

Factors that may affect the performance of mutual funds' portfolios of equities and bonds are general economic conditions, interest rates movements, political issues, corporate profits, jobs and unemployment conditions, the state of the economy in other countries abroad, the antic-

Asset Class Returns: 20-Year Snapshot | PMC Research Analysis

ENVESTNET® PMC

Asset Class Indices

- Cash – Citi Treasury 3-Month T-Bill
- Commodities – Bloomberg Commodity TR USD
- Diversified Portfolio[3]
- Emerging Markets – MSCI Emerging Markets Index
- High Yield – BarCap U.S. Corporate High Yield Index
- International Equity – MSCI EAFE Index
- Large Cap Core – Russell 1000 Index
- Large Cap Growth – Russell 1000 Growth Index
- Large Cap Value – Russell 1000 Value Index
- Mid Cap – Russell Mid Cap Index
- Munis – BarCap Municipal Index
- REITs – Dow Jones U.S. Select REIT Index
- Small Cap – Russell 2000 Index
- Top 200 – Russell Top 200 Index
- U.S. Agg – BarCap U.S. Agg Bond Index

Source: Morningstar Direct index returns. The information provided is for informational and educational purposes only. It is not intended as and should not be used to provide investment advice and does not address or account for individual investor circumstances. The asset classes described above may not be suitable for all investors and investors should first consult with an investment advisor before investing. Past performance is not indicative of future performance. Indices are unmanaged and their returns assume reinvestment of dividends and do not reflect any fees or expenses. It is not possible to invest directly in an index. Diversification does not ensure a profit or protect against a loss.

[1] Return for MSCI EM GR USD from inception date (1/1/1999) to 12/31/2015.

[3] The Diversified Portfolio is a moderate allocation blend portfolio (60%/40%) with the following allocations: 13% Russell 1000 Value; 9% Russell 1000 Growth; 12% Russell 2000; 17% MSCI EAFE; 4% MSCI Emerging Markets; 5% Dow Jones U.S. Select REIT; 40% BarCap U.S. Agg Bond.

FOR ONE-ON-ONE USE WITH A CLIENT'S FINANCIAL ADVISOR ONLY. NOT FOR GENERAL DISTRIBUTION.

© 2016 Envestnet, Inc. All rights reserved

150

ENVESTNET PMC

Fixed Income Asset Class Returns: 10-Year Snapshot
(ending December 31, 2015)

Rank	2006	2007	2008	2009	2010	2011	2012	2013	2014	2015
1	Barclays US High Yield 11.85%	Barclays US TIPS 11.64%	Barclays US Treasury 13.74%	Barclays US High Yield 58.21%	Barclays US High Yield 15.12%	Barclays US TIPS 13.56%	Barclays US High Yield 15.81%	Barclays US High Yield 7.44%	Barclays Municipal 9.05%	Barclays Municipal 3.30%
2	Barclays Global Aggregate 6.64%	Barclays Global Aggregate 9.48%	Barclays US MBS 8.34%	Barclays US Credit 16.04%	Barclays US Credit 8.47%	Barclays Municipal 10.70%	Barclays US Credit 9.37%	Barclays US Govt/Credit 1-3 Yr 0.64%	Barclays US Credit 7.53%	Barclays US MBS 1.51%
3	Barclays US MBS 5.22%	Barclays US Treasury 9.01%	Barclays US Govt/Credit 5.70%	Barclays Municipal 12.91%	Barclays US Govt/Credit 6.59%	Barclays US Treasury 9.81%	Barclays US TIPS 6.98%	Citi 3 Mon T-Bill 0.05%	Barclays US MBS 6.08%	Barclays US Interm Govt/Credit 1.07%
4	Barclays Municipal 4.84%	Barclays US Interm Govt/Credit 7.39%	Barclays US Aggregate 5.24%	Barclays US TIPS 11.41%	Barclays US Aggregate 6.54%	Barclays US Govt/Credit 8.74%	Barclays Municipal 6.78%	Barclays US Interm Govt/Credit -0.86%	Barclays US Govt/Credit 6.01%	Barclays US Govt/Credit 0.84%
5	Citi 3 Mon T-Bill 4.76%	Barclays US Govt/Credit 7.23%	Barclays US Interm Govt/Credit 5.08%	Barclays Global Aggregate 6.93%	Barclays US TIPS 6.31%	Barclays US Credit 8.35%	Barclays US Govt/Credit 4.82%	Barclays US MBS -1.41%	Barclays US Aggregate 5.97%	Barclays US Govt/Credit 1-3 Yr 0.65%
6	Barclays US Govt/Credit 1-3 Yr 4.25%	Barclays US Aggregate 6.97%	Barclays US Govt/Credit 1-3 Yr 4.97%	Barclays US Aggregate 5.93%	Barclays US Interm Govt/Credit 5.89%	Barclays US Aggregate 7.84%	Barclays Global Aggregate 4.32%	Barclays US Credit -2.01%	Barclays US Treasury 5.05%	Barclays US Aggregate 0.55%
7	Barclays US Aggregate 4.33%	Barclays US MBS 6.90%	Barclays Global Aggregate 4.79%	Barclays US MBS 5.89%	Barclays US Treasury 5.87%	Barclays US MBS 6.23%	Barclays US Aggregate 4.21%	Barclays US Aggregate -2.02%	Barclays US TIPS 3.64%	Barclays US Credit 0.15%
8	Barclays US Credit 4.26%	Barclays US Govt/Credit 1-3 Yr 6.83%	Citi 3 Mon T-Bill 1.80%	Barclays US Interm Govt/Credit 5.24%	Barclays Global Aggregate 5.54%	Barclays US Interm Govt/Credit 5.80%	Barclays US Interm Govt/Credit 3.89%	Barclays US Govt/Credit -2.35%	Barclays US Interm Govt/Credit 3.13%	Citi 3 Mon T-Bill 0.03%
9	Barclays US Interm Govt/Credit 4.08%	Barclays US Credit 5.11%	Barclays US TIPS -2.35%	Barclays US Govt/Credit 4.52%	Barclays US MBS 5.37%	Barclays Global Aggregate 5.64%	Barclays US MBS 2.59%	Barclays Municipal -2.55%	Barclays US High Yield 2.45%	Barclays US Credit -0.77%
10	Barclays US Govt/Credit 3.78%	Citi 3 Mon T-Bill 4.74%	Barclays Municipal -2.47%	Barclays US Govt/Credit 1-3 Yr 3.82%	Barclays US Govt/Credit 1-3 Yr 2.80%	Barclays US High Yield 4.98%	Barclays US Treasury 1.99%	Barclays Global Aggregate -2.60%	Barclays US Govt/Credit 1-3 Yr 0.77%	Barclays US TIPS -1.44%
11	Barclays US Treasury 3.08%	Barclays Municipal 3.36%	Barclays US Credit -3.08%	Citi 3 Mon T-Bill 0.16%	Barclays Municipal 2.38%	Barclays US Govt/Credit 1-3 Yr 1.59%	Barclays US Govt/Credit 1-3 Yr 1.26%	Barclays US Treasury -2.75%	Barclays Global Aggregate 0.59%	Barclays Global Aggregate -3.15%
12	Barclays US TIPS 0.41%	Barclays US High Yield 1.87%	Barclays US High Yield -26.16%	Barclays US Treasury -3.57%	Citi 3 Mon T-Bill 0.13%	Citi 3 Mon T-Bill 0.08%	Citi 3 Mon T-Bill 0.07%	Barclays US TIPS -8.61%	Citi 3 Mon T-Bill 0.03%	Barclays US High Yield -4.47%

management that may include real estate, commodities, private equity, endowments, and other creative investment philosophies and styles that may not be available to certain investors without the access professionally managed accounts can provide. In addition, a financial advisor will have more flexibility to manage the portfolio and to make proper changes as it becomes essential to the client's needs at different stages of the client's financial plan over time.

Finally, through these plans, financial advisors would have access to specific research tools to help manage the client portfolio. These research capabilities are different from one financial advisor to the next, but it is essential assistance in properly managing a portfolio. This does not guarantee that the performance of the investment will be better or worse, but it does provide access to opportunities and options, along with increased flexibility to explore and implement these options with the added insights that are available from these expanded research tools.

ANNUITIES AND WHY THEY EXIST

"Annuities are contracts that provide periodic payments for an agreed-upon span of time. They include "annuities certain," which provide periodic payouts for a fixed number of years, and "life annuities," which provide such payouts for the duration of one or more persons' (the annuitants') lives. The principal insurance role of annuities is to indemnify individuals against the risk of outliving their resources.

"Consider the choices confronting a retiree who has accumulated assets by saving over time, through inheritance, or as a result of company contributions to a pension plan. Assume that he expects no future income other than the return on his capital and that he has no desire to leave a be-

ipated effects of all of these factors on the US economy, and many other uncertainties that may occur on any given day. One of the most volatile factors that may affect the value of securities in mutual funds today is the impact of terrorist attacks or deteriorating international conditions in the Middle East and other regions of the world.

Classes of Mutual Funds

There are A share class of mutual funds, and C share class of funds. B share class of funds have gone by the wayside due to the costs and deferred sales charges; they are no longer deemed to be appropriate for sale. So now only A class and C class funds are being offered in general retail accounts of mutual funds. Class A shares generally include a front-end sales load that would be charged to compensate the financial advisor. These loads can range up to 5% or even 6% depending on the amount of investment that is made by the client. The higher the investment amount the lower the load, which is also referred to as the "breakpoint discount." Class C shares have a deferred sales load and usually charge a 1% fee if the funds are liquidated within the first twelve months the shares are owned. Annual expense ratios are generally higher for class C versus class A shares. There are other classes of shares physicians can include in their portfolios of mutual funds, depending on one's investment advisor and financial institution, or the amount of money the investor is interested in investing. Large investors may be able to purchase such alternative classes as Net Asset Value (without payment of a sales load) or even institutional class of shares, which also lower costs for the investor. This is referred to as a "breakpoint," and the more an investor invests, the more discount he or she will receive based on the dollar amount invested. In general terms an investment that exceeds a certain amount (usually $250,000 or more) reaches such a breakpoint, and there are discounts that apply to class A shares purchased in amounts exceeding this threshold. Also, institutional share classes may apply to certain types of investors, which may include large corporations or other big investors whose investments total more than a certain amount. Institutional share classes may also include group retirement plans, which, depending on the precise account type and amount that is invested, can offer different share classes to their customers if they so choose. Again, the best answer to questions about these sophisticated types of investment instruments will most likely be found with the help of a qualified professional financial advisor.

Types of Mutual Funds

Beyond the division of mutual funds into classes, they are also categorized by the types of securities they contain. Some may include large companies, mid-size companies, small companies, bonds, international companies, global (US and international companies), and different sectors, such as real estate, manufacturers, or other sectors. Funds are also categorized as open-ended or closed-end mutual funds. Closed-end funds are historic ancestors of what we consider mutual funds to be today; they are defined in advance in terms of the total value of the fund and a fixed number of shares. Once they are sold, the closed-end mutual fund is essentially traded like a stock on a stock exchange. Open-end funds have no limit on the number of shares that can be issued, nor on the number of investors who can purchase shares. Investors wishing to sell their shares in open-end funds can sell them back to fund managers. There are also alternative style funds, which may have different advantages depending on the investor's need and financial situation. These may include ETFs (Exchange Traded Funds), which are mutual funds that trade like stocks and have unique tax treatments. Unlike mutual funds, ETFs can incur capital gains or income taxes from the funds themselves.

PROFESSIONALLY MANAGED ACCOUNTS

These are available to investment advisors who have a certain level of experience or special securities licenses, allowing them to charge a fee for their investment advice. The client gets access to a more advanced and sophisticated style of investments. Most of these accounts don't have back end or front end load, depending on the plan and investment amounts. But they do have additional fees charged by the advisor and the financial institutions involved. These types of accounts have opened up a whole new world to the investment community. In this type of account, an investor may have access to certain classes of mutual funds or portfolio managers to which they would normally not have access. Some of these investments may typically have high minimum investment requirements, but there are ways in which professionally managed accounts can cause these minimums to be waived or consolidated in order to offer access to a group of asset classes or portfolio managers, or to accommodate certain investment styles. For example, an individual investor may not have access to an institutional share class of investments or mutual funds; these share classes carry extremely low fees and are offered to large institutional investors. But they may be available in a professionally managed account without an upfront or backend load.

An investor may also have access to specific sector funds, tax managed portfolios, or other unique and alternative styles of investment

quest. How should this individual deplete his assets each year? If he knew for certain how long he would live, this retiree could compute the time profile of consumption that would just exhaust his wealth when he died. But the fact that the individual does not know his date of death complicates the choice of a consumption profile. If he consumes relatively little in the first few years of retirement, he will make adequate provision for a very long life. There is a chance, however, that he will die with a large sum of remaining capital. Alternatively, if the individual consumes aggressively in the near term, the prospect looms of having to reduce consumption later if he lives longer than expected.

"Annuities solve the retiree's consumption problem. In return for an initial capital payment, he is assured of receiving a constant income stream for the remainder of his life. The annuity provider can pool mortality risk across similar individuals and thereby can, with the principal left behind by those who died sooner than expected, insure those who live unexpectedly long. As a result, the annuitant's payout from the annuity contract can, in theory, exceed what he could earn if he invested the amount of his annuity premium and then consumed only the income flow.

"Annuities are sometimes referred to as 'reverse life insurance.' With life insurance, the policy holder pays the insurer each year until he or she dies, after which the insurance company pays a lump sum to the insured's beneficiaries. With annuities, the lump-sum payment is from the annuitant to the insurance company before the annuity payout begins, and the annuitant receives regular payouts from the insurer until death.

"Most annuity contracts have an 'accumulation phase' and a 'liquidation phase.' During the accumulation phase, capital builds up; this capital is dispersed during the liquidation phase…

"Annuities have historically been offered by insurance companies, which pool the mortality risk across many individuals and thereby achieve a more predictable cash flow than if they offered an annuity to only one individual. The same principles that underpin risk reduction in life insurance sales apply to the provision of annuity payouts. The annuity supplier must have sufficient capital and be sufficiently long-lived to ensure that annuity payouts will still be paid if the annuitant lives for many years."[1]

The history of annuities actually goes back much further than that of mutual funds. Annuities can trace their origins all the way to Ancient Rome, and a contract called an *annua*, in which the buyer paid an agreed-on up-front payment in return for a stream of payments for a fixed number of years. Ancient Roman buyers used these *annuae* to provide retirement income; sellers gambled that they would earn a profit by repaying less money over time than they received in advance. Because necessity is the mother of invention, *annuae* also gave rise to actuarial tables, said to have been invented by a Roman scholar named Ulpianis in 222 C.E. His work to predict how long, on average, an entire pool of *annuae* buyers might live, gave sellers a more accurate idea of the profits they might realize. For centuries, annuities were used in Europe in a variety of ways. Kings sold annuities to fund wars and construction projects; the Church used them for similar purposes; and on a smaller scale, communities used them to share in investments to benefit the common good. Annuities were popular with wealthy Europeans who saw them as more reliable investments with a stronger likelihood of return.

The first American annuity is older than the United States itself; in 1759, the Corporation for the Poor and Distressed Presbyterian Ministers

1 "History of Annuities in the United States"; James M. Poterba; NBER Working Paper No. 6001; April 1997; JEL Nos. G22, D91; *Aging, Asset Pricing, Corporate Finance and Public Economics*

and Distressed Widows and Children of Ministers sold annuities to serving ministers in return for the promise of guaranteed payments to them or their survivors in the future. During the Revolutionary War, annuities were also sold to provide for soldiers who fought for independence. Andrew Carnegie founded what would become the Teacher's Insurance and Annuity Association in 1905, and in 1952, with the founding of TIAA-CREF, the educators' retirement fund that still exists today, began offering the first group-variable deferred annuity. Investors in this fund, like holders of open-end mutual funds, can invest an unlimited amount of money; the advantage for TIAA-CREF annuity owners is that, in 1986, the federal government allowed these annuities to earn money on a tax-deferred basis.[2]

Annuities are popular because they provide predictable and stable income streams for specified periods of time; risk-averse investors see them as an attractive alternative to the uncertainties of the stock market. Since annuity payment streams may be defined to last anywhere from five years to a lifetime stream of payments, they shift the risk of outliving the income stream from the buyer (or, in other words, the investor) to the seller (in today's economy, the insurance provider). Annuities have become more popular as human life expectancies have increased, and as we have witnessed the high volatility of market conditions, including the 2001 and 2008 market crashes or "corrections."

Consistent with the long history of annuities providing for people who are "poor" or "distressed," many institutions offer some sort of annuity contracts to their employees, to be paid out upon their retirement, or in the event of their death, to their survivors. Teachers, non-profit institutions, and churches may offer these annuities, which are also called 403(b) plans due to their IRS classification as tax-deferred salary deferral retire-

---

2 http://www.annuity.org/annuities/history/

ment plans. Even the federal government may offer some sort of annuity payment options for their employees and surviving beneficiaries.

There are different types of annuities as they have evolved to fill gaps in the financial needs of different individuals. There are fixed annuities, which have very low principal risk when compared to the performance of a stock market; however, it is worth noting that this risk is never truly "zero," because it is always dependent on the financial stability of the insurance company guaranteeing these annuities. Variable annuities, which allow investors to choose their own underlying investments, introduce the concept of annuity "subaccounts." In these cases, the investor accepts the risk of fluctuations in the market through their underlying subaccounts. More recently, the idea of Index Annuities emerged. These are a combination of variable and fixed accounts, allowing some level of participation in the market through portfolio-based indexes they offer. In most cases, these annuities protect the principal from losses, while they also allow participation in the upside potential of the indexes they include, and limit the risk of the annuity holder's principal. There are many moving parts and a high level of sophistication in these products, and investors are encouraged to seek the advice of a qualified financial professional who is trained and experienced in annuities and similar instruments. It is also important that this advisor doesn't have any conflict of interest or loyalty to any specific plan or insurance carrier. We further suggest that you do your own research and see how these plans may affect your financial security (in both a positive or negative way); you should never rely solely on the advice of your financial consultant/advisor, CPA, or (especially) relatives and friends. People who are not highly trained and qualified in these products may not fully understand the advantages or disadvantages of a specific plan. Many people—qualified or not—have heard something negative or positive about a plan, and they may impose their beliefs into others, which may end up to be counterproductive in developing a secure financial plan.[3]

Annuities may have been around for centuries, but they have evolved rapidly in number and type, and in their prevalence among investors, since the 1930s. Since World War II, corporate pension plans have represented the largest share of the American annuity market, and with the rise of variable annuities, they have extended their "reach" in the market to include investment features that are similar to mutual funds. The popularity of annuities in general, and the continued growth of tax-deferred annuities since the 1980s, have fueled a long-standing debate about which financial institutions should be allowed to sell annuities. Traditional restrictions on the sale of annuities by insurance companies only, due to annuities' "risk sharing and indemnification qualities," were relaxed in the 1990s, and now "annuity-like products" can be purchased from some banks, although the issue is still officially unresolved. The relationship between annuities and federal programs for the elderly—specifically Medicare and Social Security, which some analysts have likened to annuities in their structure—is also the subject of much discussion, particularly if these programs are going to be reduced in terms of the benefits they provide in the future.

When considering the purchase of an annuity, we always recommend checking on the financial stability of the carrier. This includes the health of the overall company, and also its record of consistency in payments to its customers. Financial advisors like ourselves routinely provide this service. Disclosures about financial stability and payment history are publicly available, but individuals without financial expertise may need help in interpreting some aspects of these reports. Without a stable carrier, annuities may not be the low-risk investment instrument we normally consider them

3 http://www.sec.gov/answers/annuity.htm

to be. Still, annuities are an enormously popular investment tool, and are most popular with older individual investors—those over fifty-five years old. Annuities are widely recognized by both corporate managers and individuals facing retirement as a way to provide reliable income; we will revisit this topic again in Chapter 11, "Retirement Planning."

Physicians—and everyone, really—need to be open-minded when it comes to financial planning, and should explore all potential financial products and strategies, including annuities. They should not ignore financial products of any kind that can play an important role in their financial plan, just because they may have heard something negative from a friend, relative, or acquaintance. Other people's experiences and understanding of these complex financial products are not an accurate method for making a decision on anyone's individual financial plan. One must explore what these financial products will do for oneself and select the best method to help accomplish the goals and objectives, including risk management, in developing this plan.

CASH MANAGEMENT CONSIDERATIONS

When anyone, physician or otherwise, is developing a personal investment plan, cash management is a consideration that cannot be overlooked. Beyond the main cash management goal of never running out of it, there are other concerns, some of which we have already discussed. Making sure there will be enough cash on hand to deal with unforeseen emergencies, or to fund non-financial needs like college or children's wedding expenses, is a priority that is more important than going after the maximum return on cash on hand. Tying up liquid assets in a way that limits one's ability to handle these needs for cash is not an acceptable investment strategy, regardless of the return.

Similarly, when it comes to debt, borrowing money, or keeping personal debt "on the books" while pursuing investment returns, may not be as wise as paying the debt first. This is not always the case, of course; mortgages and car payments may be acceptable debt given their value in providing secure housing and transportation for an individual physician and his or her family. But an honest evaluation of current cash accounts, and the best way to manage them, is an important foundation for any investment strategy. Don't miss the opportunity to take this necessary first step before shopping for mutual funds, annuities, or other investment opportunities.

Having enough cash reserve is a sort of personal first line of defense. There needs to be enough cash available so that no matter what happens in a person's financial life, he or she will not be required to tap into other assets, including a retirement plan or other financial account that has been established to support a different part of the financial plan.

This issue may not seem that serious, but in down times such as 2001 and 2008 where not only the stock market but the economy as a whole took a turn for the worse, many people were forced to liquidate their retirement accounts and other assets. In some cases, they lost their homes due to foreclosure due to not having enough cash on hand. In order to avoid financial hardships like these, it is highly recommended to have a reasonable amount of funds available in cash for emergencies. There is no set "rule" on what level of funds needs to be available for emergencies; this is a matter for individual consideration. I am a financial planner, but not knowing the circumstances of each reader of this book, I will not provide general information that may not help—or in fact may hurt—a particular individual. Financial planning should always be seen as a dialogue with a trusted advisor, and never as a lecture.

Chapter 11

WEALTH ACCUMULATION II–
RETIREMENT PLANNING

RETIREMENT PLANNING IS A CONCEPT that many people believe is almost interchangeable with individual financial planning, one of the key subjects of this book. In many ways, that's a strange fact, since despite the importance you'd think this misunderstanding would bring to the idea of planning for retirement, very few Americans have actually made a real plan for maintaining an adequate level of income after they stop earning a paycheck. Even more noteworthy is the rapidly-changing definition many of us have for exactly what retirement is.

Financial advisors like us often start conversations with our clients by asking the question, "What does retirement mean to you?" It's not a trick question, but we get a surprising range of answers. "Not working!" is one of the most common. "Doing all the things I've always wanted to do in my life but didn't have the time," is another. "Collecting my pension" is an answer we don't hear very much anymore, since most corporate pension plans have all but disappeared in the past few decades. "Keeping money coming in to support myself and my spouse" is perhaps the answer we like the most, because it is, in fact, what we professionals believe the goal of any retirement plan ought to be.

RETIREMENT PLANNING BEGINS LIKE ANY OTHER ASPECT OF A FINANCIAL PLAN

Because this is a book for physicians, there is a strong likelihood that most readers will have the means to accumulate enough savings to support the last and best answer in our previous paragraph, which in some ways makes the challenge of retirement planning for physicians easier. But in other ways, the larger amounts of money to allocate for retirement planning can also mean making a bigger mistake without proper design, or without regularly updated guidance on how to manage a long-term plan in a rapidly-changing world. Like most other topics included in this book—*What They Don't Teach You in Medical & Dental School*, one of the biggest mistakes a doctor can make is failing to take the key first steps toward creating a successful plan. We can't remind readers enough to start by taking stock of your own unique situation. What are your sources of revenue? What are your expenses? How much do you want to save for short-term priorities, for unforeseen emergencies, and for long-term investments like a home, experiences that are important for you to have during your life, for other non-financial goals like your children's college education, weddings, perhaps a family summer outpost on the seashore or in the mountains, or... retirement? Can you allocate your income to support all of these goals, or, if you can't, are there other options, like insurance policies against unforeseen expenses or additional sources of revenue, which can help you get there? What are the risks that might keep you from reaching all of these goals, and what can be done about them? Since no plan can reduce all risks to zero, which of these risks are tolerable for you, and which must be guarded against at all costs?

These questions are important for every aspect of a physician's (or anyone else's) financial plan, but they often get the most attention when they are asked in terms of planning for one's retirement. And so we are asking them here. But please do yourself a favor. Read these questions again, add any others you think are important for your own retirement plan, remove the ones you don't think need to be part of such a plan for you and your family, and remember the final list. Write down that list and save it, if you haven't already done so, for it will be the best first step in any element of your financial plan you will develop throughout your life. Yes, it's that important.

But for now, we'll concentrate on retirement planning. It, too, begins with this vital first step. Once you've answered for yourself what you'd like your retirement to be like, when you'd like it to begin, who else is involved in your plans for retirement, and other considerations that are unique and meaningful to your own idea of retirement, you can begin weighing options, reviewing different paths that lead to your goals, and choosing the one that's best for you. Essentially, after defining your vision of what you want your own retirement to be, your second step is to make sure you have created a plan through which you will have both the assets and the income to support that uniquely personal concept of retirement for all the years you, and those with whom you choose to share it, will enjoy together. That's it! The rest are details. This book can help introduce you to many of these details, such as using some of the investment vehicles we've discussed in previous chapters, defining and understanding risks more fully in order to plan for their possible impact on your plan, and looking at a few specific retirement vehicles to explain how they can be used—or why they shouldn't be used—in a given individual's plan.

RETIREMENT PLANNING IS INCOME PLANNING

Like we mentioned earlier, today's concept of retirement is changing rapidly. For many individuals, particularly skilled and experienced individuals like physicians, retirement no longer means a last day at work, a big going-away party with co-workers, a gold watch, and a chance to make an eloquent speech thanking everyone for making your career the wonderful experience it has been. As a matter of fact, all of these events can be included in your plan for retirement, except one. You probably will never stop "working." Sharing your knowledge as a teacher, and providing mentoring guidance for younger medical professionals can always be part of your future, as will a limited amount of income associated with these services, if you want to do that. It's just another of the many choices and options you will have for a next career phase that may not be as dramatic a change as what we previously called retirement, but one that will certainly be yours to define and enjoy.

Still, this is more about the non-financial goal of remaining active and productive later in life; the income a physician might earn from consulting or teaching during retirement may not be significant enough to offset the need to accumulate enough money to pay for many years free of financial worry, and in any case, it probably shouldn't be. It's just that physicians, like politicians, often become more valuable with every passing year, and are most appreciated for the contributions they make long after professionals in other fields have stopped being productive. Our job in writing this book—and in encouraging you to seek the help of a trusted financial advisor in planning for your retirement—is to help you make the big choices that will define what you mean as a successful retirement, and to then help you with the nuts-and-bolts strategies and tactics to implement a plan that will get you there.

Retirement planning, as we see it, is about income planning. Simply put, it means making sure the checks keep coming in when an individual stops working. Traditional means for doing this, such as pension plans, which are disappearing; or investing in the stock market alone, which can include levels of risk that are unacceptable for people needing assurance they will not run out of money late in life; or more "modern" instruments like 401(k) and other defined contribution plans, which individuals might not fund properly to provide for the retirement they have defined for themselves, are no longer enough. Combinations of various instruments, including some that might be surprising to most people, are becoming the norm in creating the "income plan" that we want to use in place of the old concept of a "retirement plan."

Your income plan will have two phases. The first, and most immediate part, is the "accumulation phase," in which you take current income and place it in one or more investment instruments to save for the second phase, the "distribution phase," in which you withdraw funds from these instruments to provide income in your retirement years. Note that these phases are similar to the "accumulation phase" and "liquidation phase" included in the description of annuities earlier in this section of the book. In both annuities and retirement planning, the combination of these two phases requires great planning; many individuals don't understand the various aspects of income planning, or how to be sure they have arrived at a strategy for each of the two phases of their plans. The goals, of course, are to be sure that enough funds are present at the end of the accumulation phase, and that the withdrawal rate during the distribution phase doesn't drain these funds too quickly, or, alternatively, too slowly. It's just as important for a retired individual to spend enough to enjoy retirement so there isn't too much left over at the end of his or her life as it is important for the retiree not to "outlive" his or her plan.

THE ACCUMULATION PHASE: TYPES OF RETIREMENT PLANS

The two major categories of retirement plans are referred to as either "defined benefit" or "defined contribution" plans. Defined benefit plans, which place the risk of payment on the corporation or government body offering the plan, are becoming less available to employees with every passing day. Either they are no longer offered, given the unpredictable risk they pose for corporate managers, or—worse—they are terminated after retirees have become dependent upon them due to bankruptcy of the sponsoring organization. We have all read about the sad effects of such "downsizing" of benefits to employees of large companies like General Motors, or governments like the City of Detroit. It is unwise for anyone to depend on these sorts of plans, even when they are offered, because there is an increasing risk that these funds will not be available during retirement, no matter what is promised. That is why the shift to defined contribution plans, in which employees or individual plan holders make their own investments into accounts they own, has been so significant in the past few decades. Because the trend in today's world is overwhelmingly in favor of defined contribution plans, we will concentrate our discussion on them and not on the defined benefit plans that are becoming increasingly rare.

Most physicians who are employed by hospitals and other health care organizations do have some sort of company-sponsored retirement plan, but even if they are defined contribution plans, they may not be the most optimized plan designs as there are many different styles of group retirement plans. Other physicians who own their own practices may also provide for themselves in the employee retirement plans their human resources staff have designed, but these, too, may suffer from the same less-than-optimal characteristics as other group plans. Group plans may include 401(k) plans, 403(b) plans, 457 plans, and variations such as simple IRAs, simple 401(k) plans, and Roth 401(k) plans. Other retirement instruments companies may choose to offer can be profit sharing plans, and, of course, traditional defined benefit pension plans.

The IRS lists fifteen different types of retirement plans for individuals and families to consider. These include:

- Individual Retirement Arrangements (IRAs)
- Roth IRAs
- 401(k) Plans
- 401(b) Plans
- Simple IRA Plans
- SEP Plans
- SARSEP Plans
- Payroll Deduction IRAs
- Profit Sharing Plans
- Defined Benefit Plans
- Money Purchase Plans
- Employee Stock Ownership Plans (ESOPs)
- Government Plans
- 457 Plans
- 409A Nonqualified Deferred Compensation Plans

We won't go into specifics on each of these fifteen official definitions; instead, we recommend you talk with your financial advisor to determine which of these are best for you and your practice. Some decisions about the best plan for a small business are related to the number of employees that business has; others are related to the way the business is structured; and others are related to the individual preferences of the owner(s) in terms of benefits they choose to provide. A qualified financial advisor is a good start, but in some cases, a physician practice owner may want to engage the services of an independent third-party administrator who is qualified to help make these choices, and to then assist in managing them going forward.[1]

Since individual retirement accounts, also referred to as IRAs, have a maximum limit of $5,000 to $6,000 per year, most physicians and business owners turn to other 401(k) plans that offer much higher limits for making contributions. Generally speaking, these higher-limit 401(k) plans may allow for contributions as high as $18,000 per year (note that this figure is subject to annual adjustments and/or indexing by the government), and individuals over the age of fifty may be eligible for catch-up provisions to add additional money for their retirement. Although there are requirements and costs associated with setting up 401(k) plans, over the years these costs have been reduced due to competition, transparency regarding fee disclosures now mandated by law, and the fact that the government is sincerely trying to promote business owners and individuals to save money for their retirement.

1 http://www.irs.gov/Retirement-Plans/Plan-Participant,-Employee/Definitions and http://www.irs.gov/Retirement-Plans/Plan-Sponsor/Types-of-Retirement-Plans-1

RESPONSIBILITIES OF PLAN ADMINISTRATORS

Physicians/business owners need to be aware that they have several responsibilities as fiduciaries and sponsors of such plans. Most recently the department of labor has released requirements and procedures that business owners must follow in order to provide reasonable and legitimate retirement plans for themselves and their employees. In light of some recent problems with a variety of different 401(k) plans and major corporations that have been the subjects of lawsuits from their employees, the government is requiring providers of 401(k) plans, financial advisors, and those who are considered to be fiduciaries to follow specific procedures to ensure the safety of their employees and to make sure their plans are in compliance with these new requirements. Plan sponsors and fiduciaries must work closely with their qualified financial advisors, third-party administrators, and tax advisors to ensure that the structures required by law are followed, so that in an event of an audit, or problems that may arise as a result of an employee complaint, their activities in managing the plan can be justified and documented as following proper procedures.

The main process of implementing a 401(k) plan is to first review and evaluate proposals, to see which type of plan and formulas may be suitable and to pick the best option for your specific situation. Then, different plans and providers must be compared and evaluated to ensure that the services, investment options, expenses, and all other related benefits offered to the employees are priced within a reasonable range. These evaluations must continue on a regular basis to ensure that they are still within the reasonable range, and that they offer suitable investment selections with reasonable expenses.

Since the basic platform of today's group retirement plans are 401(k) plans, those who wish to add additional funds and accumulate more money for their retirement may need to implement additional plans in combination with these existing 401(k)s. These additional plans may include features such as matching, which allows the employer to match employee contributions at a certain percentage level. Some of these matching provisions may be required by law and some may not; it is important to have a qualified plan administrator who can evaluate these plans from beginning to end, and who can also conduct compliance reviews on an annual basis to make sure the plan remains in compliance with IRS and other government regulatory requirements. Another feature companies may include is profit sharing, which is an added benefit that can add additional contributions to the plan, to help the employer and employees save more money for retirement, while enjoying additional tax benefits through tax deductions the plan provides. These benefits will be taxable in future years, when distributions begin. It is also important to note that profit sharing contributions are not mandatory; the business owner/employer decides whether to make additional contributions each year.

Finally, if the business owner/physician wishes to add even more dollars to the retirement plan, he or she may choose a combination plan, which may include the addition of a variation to traditional defined benefit pension plans. Combination plans focus on providing a defined benefit for some future years as opposed to a defined contribution which employees can make each year up to certain limits. Because combination plans are classified as defined benefit plans and not defined contribution plans, they can have higher limits—in some cases much higher limits—on what an individual may contribute each year. Contributions and benefits are based on an employee's current age and the age at which retirement will begin, to create a defined annual benefit upon retirement. These plans are complicated and may have unique requirements; physicians and clients are advised to seek the expertise of qualified individuals who understand these sorts of plans.

Given the fact that many physicians are self-employed, there may be options in such individual retirement instruments as the good old IRA and Roth IRA. Contributions for these plans are much lower, but for those who are not able to make higher contributions, they can be good options. It's important to check with a tax advisor to determine eligibility for these and other individual retirement plans. Annuities are also important elements of income plans we recommend for physicians to use in accumulating money for retirement; given their history in providing predictable income streams for thousands of years, and recent additions of variable risk annuities and those offering tax-deferred income, there are a number of attractive options to add to a retirement income-generating portfolio. Some annuities are available to teachers and employees of educational institutions, and others are available to nonprofit organizations and their employees—like hospitals and other community health care organizations. Our point is that physicians may have access to an unanticipated wide variety of income planning opportunities, which, taken together, can offer a range of options balancing risk and return, or favorable tax consequences. Making sure all of these opportunities are explored for their value in the accumulation phase of a physician's income planning is a great way to build a solid retirement plan, one which a financial advisor can help make even more successful.

THE DISTRIBUTION PHASE: EXPENSE PLANNING, AND MANAGING RISK

Planning for the distribution phase of a retirement income plan is much like the "nuts-and-bolts" phase of a larger financial plan. We've already defined the type of retirement we want; the next step is to calculate the annual expenses associated with living the life we've defined for this phase of our career, and making sure there's enough income to cover these anticipated expenses. There's one important difference when it comes to retirement planning, though, and that is the difficult arrival at a balance between spending enough money to enjoy our retirement years without distributing all our revenue and running out of cash before we die. Alternatively, we don't want to restrict the enjoyment of our retirement years and have a miserable time, leaving behind a large sum of money we intended to spend. Guessing at the number of years each of us will live is a disturbing calculation, and may in itself alone be the best reason for consulting a financial advisor, who can help us do this objectively. First and most important is the risk of running out of money by taking either too much distribution, or excess withdrawal risks. Many people don't understand the distribution phase of retirement planning. Most financial advisors show or project a specific rate of return (ROR) during retirement, and if this ROR holds true, then the plan may work. But markets don't generate the same rates of return every year, and if one takes distributions out, thinking that these funds will last a lifetime, then he or she may be disappointed if the markets don't provide returns as high as those that were projected, and on which the entire plan was formulated. In other words, care should be taken in creating and especially in managing a retirement plan to ensure that the client isn't taking too much money in the event that the projected—and necessary—rate of return needed is not reached. Similar problems can be caused by the impact of inflation; retirement income planning should include some sort of inflation hedge to handle potential increases in expenses over time associated with rising costs of living. In a way, this is similar to the cash management considerations we saw in other aspects of our individual financial plans.

Beyond actuarial considerations, calculations regarding withdrawals based on them, and cash management issues related to issues such as inflation, our retirement income plans also need to consider risk factors including taxes, unexpected expenses, increased spending on travel and other leisure activities, emergencies, rising costs of health care, long-term care, family emergencies and assistance, and other potential needs for cash. Other increases in expenses that people face in retirement may also include family members and children and grandchildren who may need assistance due to unforeseen circumstances, or unanticipated increases in property taxes or household expenses that continue through retirement.

In addition, stock market fluctuations also need to be considered. Even diversified portfolios may still be subject to significant principal fluctuation, which may have a huge impact on how much an individual can take as distributions during retirement. Being over-invested in certain funds or investment vehicles, or in assets such as real estate, bring additional risks if these assets unexpectedly lose value. There are also psychological issues associated with how an individual deals with uncertainty and excess concern about short-term portfolio values and the impact of these fluctuations on planned retirement distributions. These psychological attitudes toward risk actually vary by gender, and are worth discussing in advance as a way to avoid unnecessarily risky—or risk-averse—decision making during retirement.[2]

When it comes to the distribution phase, there are also family risks to consider. Retirees may need to take care of aging parents or children who are in need of financial and/or physical assistance. Retirees may face the risk of having to care for parents or children who may need financial and

---

2 http://www.socialsecurity.gov/policy/docs/ssb/v71n4/v71n4p15.html
and http://www.dol.gov/ebsa/publications/women.html

physical assistance. The death of a spouse during retirement may cause financial hardship or the loss of anticipated income. This is particularly true with respect to Social Security; after a small death benefit, monthly payments may be reduced after the death of a primary beneficiary. Last but not least, a change in marital status may result in changes to anticipated income streams, requiring adjustments to one's retirement plan.

A FEW WORDS ABOUT SOCIAL SECURITY RETIREMENT BENEFITS

The way Social Security distributions are designed and selected can play a major impact on how much an individual or the family will receive during their lifetimes; without proper planning, this can translate to hundreds of thousands of dollars lost if filings are done improperly, or if filing deadlines are missed. These are highly complicated procedures, and people should seek the help of qualified financial professionals who understand these concepts. Unfortunately, most financial advisors or even CPAs may not be aware of some of the unique benefits and risks associated with this large and complicated government program. In some cases even the Social Security Administration doesn't provide advice on how to take distributions properly, leaving people in the dark.

Important highlighted areas include: when is the best time to file for Social Security? Is it best to file at the earliest qualified age (currently sixty-two), at full retirement age (between sixty-five and sixty-seven years old, depending on one's age), or later in life? What are the benefits for eligible children? How are payouts affected by whether an individual is single, married, widowed, divorced, widowed with eligible children, or divorced with eligible children? What is the difference between retirement benefits vs. survivor benefits?

There are also Social Security strategy and benefit options to consider, such as withdrawal of application-payback, suspension of benefits, file and suspend—enabling retroactive benefits and also enabling spousal benefits, final restricted status—for spousal benefits only, or combination strategy—final and suspend and final restricted.

Most people know that in 1983, the Social Security Administration (SSA) increased the retirement age for many Americans. Beginning with those born in 1938, the age for full retirement increases by approximately two months for each subsequent "birth year." In other words, those born in 1938 still have a retirement age of sixty-five, while those born in 1939 have a new retirement age of sixty-five and two months. This increase is maintained until it reaches sixty-six for those born in 1943, and this age continues at the same level—sixty-six years and no additional months—for everyone born from 1943 through 1954. Those born in 1955 can retire at age sixty-six and two months; this same two-month increase continues through those born in 1960, when the retirement age reaches sixty-seven. For everyone born in 1960 and later, the full retirement age remains at sixty-seven. Early retirement remains at age sixty-two for everyone.

The SSA has also provided additional annual retirement benefits for those who retire later than their full retirement year (up to age seventy). The following chart from the Social Security Administration website shows the percentage increase in monthly benefits a retiree can expect to receive for every year he or she delays retirement:

Increase for Delayed Retirement

Year of Birth*	Yearly Rate of Increase	Monthly Rate of Increase
1933-1934	5.5%	11/24 of 1%
1935-1936	6.0%	1/2 of 1%
1937-1938	6.5%	13/24 of 1%
1939-1940	7.0%	7/12 of 1%
1941-1942	7.5%	5/8 of 1%
1943 or later	8.0%	2/3 of 1%

*Note: If you were born on January 1st,
you should refer to the rate of increase for the previous year.

RETIREMENT PLANNING WRAP-UP

Retirement planning is what many individuals believe is the main component of financial planning. Professional financial advisors believe it is only one aspect of this planning, although we don't want to judge how important it may be for any individual. After reviewing the content presented throughout this book, we leave it to the physicians/business owners who have read this far to make these judgments on their own. Whether retirement planning, navigating the many changes brought about by health care reform, or putting together risk management strategies combining insurance, cash reserves, and training of a practice's employees to minimize their likelihood of making a costly mistake is a physician's most significant take-away from this book is not the issue. Our goal is to convince physicians to approach their "favorite" financial management challenge in a methodical way, paying attention to the three primary categories of resources and tolls: risk management, wealth accumulation, and advanced planning.

And, of course, we want to state as often as possible the importance of adding the service of a qualified financial planning professional. We can help!

Chapter 12

ADVANCED PLANNING—
CREATIVE FINANCIAL TOOLS AND RESOURCES

ONCE THE BASICS OF FINANCIAL PLANNING have been established, some advanced concepts and considerations may be needed in order to create a complete personal investment plan for certain individuals and families. It may seem obvious that those who can be described in a "high wealth" category are most likely to take advantage of these advanced concepts, but experienced financial managers know this is not necessarily true. Just because certain individuals have higher incomes, it doesn't mean that they are doing all that is essential. It also doesn't mean that they've considered, or are even aware of, the advanced concepts in investment management—or financial management in general—that are available to them. In fact, most high income and high net worth physicians and individuals are busy with their day-to-day activities and businesses, and may not have the time to meet with proper professionals to perform reviews and consider strategies they might need to take advantage of their unique circumstances.

It's also possible that many people who have gathered and accumulated significant assets believe that they are doing their planning properly by simply meeting with a financial advisor with an agenda limited to the selection of optimal investment accounts. Experienced financial planners know this doesn't mean anything. Simply having an investment account doesn't mean that real financial planning has been done.

We've discussed a few of the advanced financial planning resources and tools available for physician's practices and small businesses earlier in this book. This section includes an overview of some of these advanced resources as they apply to individuals, including setting up a living trust or evaluating other forms of trust that may be appropriate, such as revocable trusts, irrevocable trusts, asset protection trusts, life insurance trusts, charitable trusts, special needs trusts, dynasty trusts, charitable remainder and annuity trusts, or qualified terminable interest property ("QTIP") trusts, and intentionally defective trusts.

ADVANCED ESTATE PLANNING, INCLUDING CHARITABLE TRUSTS AND CHARITABLE PLANNING

While they are typically more likely to be used by the very wealthy, in recent years, some financial institutions have made these same tools, or variations of them, available to people of more modest means. Estate planning is a crucial element of financial planning because, without it, significant costs associated with the settlement of an estate can reduce the value of assets intended for one's family and other heirs. In addition, without proper planning, the time required to settle an estate can become unreasonably long, delaying a family's access to these assets. And finally, there are questions of control and management of funds left by an individual to his or her family, particularly when heirs are minor children. Without clearly-defined estate planning, it is possible that control of an individual's assets may be assigned to or assumed by someone who is not qualified or trustworthy enough to manage them. A list of plans we'll introduce here (this is by no means an exhaustive summary) include:

What is a living trust and why you should have it

This type of trust assigns control of the full principal to the surviving spouse. Its main purpose is to avoid probate and the time and costs involved in this process. If required, the trust can also be used to manage the assets for beneficiaries who are not yet ready to inherit the assets outright, either because they are not yet of age, or because they lack the experience needed to be responsible investors and/or financial managers.

Holding proper title to assets and property: why this is important

At death, many states apply specific laws to define which property is fully owned by the deceased, which is jointly owned by the deceased and his/her spouse, and which is owned by the spouse (or someone else). Generally, these laws provide for property owned prior to marriage to remain the separate property of the individual owning spouse, while property earned or accumulated during marriage through the efforts of both spouses is defined as "community property," with each spouse owning half. Other property, or tenancy, is legally defined in a standard way by many states, and without proper definition of ownership, these definitions can prevent the distribution of assets as intended by an individual at the time of his or her death. It is important for the titles that define ownership of these assets to be written in such a way that allows for their intended distribution at death. Examples of the way this can be accomplished include the addition of a "right of survivorship" for community property, which allows title to automatically pass to the surviving spouse by operation of law. An example of potential difficulties is the concept of "tenancy-in-partnership," a form of ownership that creates permanent rights of ownership to each partner. In these cases, specific interest in the property owned by the partnership cannot be conveyed by one partner alone. Without modification, this type of ownership can prevent intended distribution of assets at death.

Capital gains taxes

The federal government has long made provisions to provide for more favorable (lower) tax rates for long-term capital gains, which are defined as the appreciation of the value of assets such as real estate, investments, collectibles, and other property at the end of a period vs. their value at the time the taxpayer acquired or assumed ownership of these assets. The income tax treatment of capital gains and losses is complex and often confusing. Individuals facing decisions concerning the tax implications of the sale or exchange of a capital asset, or the proper way to include such assets in an estate plan, should consult with a CPA, IRS enrolled agent, or other qualified tax professional.

Capital gains taxes are subject to rules that often allow an owner to manage their timing and impact on the owner's or his/her heirs' financial well-being. For example, because these taxes are usually levied at the time a capital asset is sold or otherwise disposed of, the year in which these taxes apply is defined by the time an owner chooses. There are also rules governing the minimum time an asset must be "held" by the owner in order to qualify for capital gains treatment, and several exclusions from taxation, such as a maximum value of real estate that is also the owner's (or his/her spouse's) primary residence. While an owner can create a sound financial plan for managing the impact of taxes on the sale or disposition of capital assets during his or her lifetime, ensuring this sort of management continues after death is a critical element of estate planning, and includes such considerations as the timing of any sales, the impact of capital gains taxes on heirs who may want to sell them, their degree of financial management experience or expertise, etc. This is why the help of a professional is so important when capital assets are included in any estate plan.

Stretch in IRA accounts

This technique provides an individual with the opportunity to leave his or her IRA accounts to dependent children. While the rules are specific enough to require careful planning (for example, the individual's IRA account(s) must be split into separate new IRA accounts, each of which names one child as the sole beneficiary, and these accounts cannot mix funds with other IRA assets), this method allows the owner to take his or her required minimum distributions (RMDs) as would be the case if he or she still owned the IRA, but at death allows for each IRA account to be inherited by the child named as beneficiary. At that time, each IRA account and its RMDs are governed by the individual life expectancy of the child who now owns the account.

Life insurance and how it is used in estate planning

Death proceeds from a life insurance policy are almost always income tax free. In fact, since 1982, federal tax law provides for an unlimited marital deduction on the transfer of ownership of assets from one spouse to another, so there is no need to plan for life insurance ownership based on taxation at the time of the first spouse's death. There is an important consideration, however, in the surviving spouse's financial plan. If the value of a life insurance policy's death benefit is significant, it can greatly increase the value of the surviving spouse's estate, and at the time of his or her death, result in substantial taxation when these assets are left to surviving children or other individuals. Setting up an irrevocable life insurance trust or ownership of the insurance policies by children or grandchildren can remove the proceeds from the insured estate, as well as the estate of the surviving spouse.

Noncitizen spouses and estate planning

While federal tax law since 1982 has provided for an unlimited marital deduction on the transfer of assets to a surviving spouse, this only applies when that surviving spouse is a United States citizen. In situations when the surviving spouse is not a U.S. citizen, there is an applicable exclusion amount that applies in all other cases. In 2015, this exclusion amount is $5,430,000. The transfer of assets from one spouse to another—by gift, for example—is not a viable solution here, since any gift in excess of $147,000 per year (as defined in 2015) will be taxable. The answer for transferring assets without tax liability in these cases lies in the establishment of a Qualified Domestic Trust (QDOT), which can receive these assets and hold them without taxation, but still allow the noncitizen spouse to control them, with certain limitations. Those limitations include the requirement that the QDOT include at least one trustee who is a U.S. citizen or domestic corporation; the U.S. trustee must be able to withhold taxes due on any distributions of the trust's principal; and the trust must be able to collect federal estate taxes as defined by law.

Special needs children

A trust established for the benefit of a special needs child can help family members provide some benefits to that child without causing him or her to lose government benefits. This is a complex financial instrument, and includes definitions of the basic needs (food, clothing, shelter) and supplementary needs (medical care, education, special equipment, telephone bills, entertainment, etc.) that can be purchased for the child by the trust. In addition, ownership of the trust is subject to other requirements. For example, parents can act as trustees, but the trust should be separate from the family's other trust(s). Beneficiaries should also be named to receive trust assets after the disabled child dies, and there needs to be a plan for how the trust will be funded and managed throughout the life of the child, particularly after the death of his or her parents.

Family limited partnerships (FLPs)

These instruments can be used to hold business, personal, or investment assets. Their purpose is to divide investment income with children in lower tax brackets in order to increase the family's net spendable income. They are also important ways for a family to ensure the transfer of family business ownership from one generation to the next. Without an FLP, federal tax law applies to the transfer of assets from "closely held businesses" in ways that can effectively prevent such a transfer; these taxes include federal estate and generation-skipping transfer taxes. FLPs have also been used to protect family assets from creditors. One of the most attractive elements of an FLP is its flexibility; unlike other estate planning strategies, an FLP's governing document can be modified to respond to changes in the family or business structure. However, it is important to note that FLPs are limited to businesses and investments involving the production of capital assets or other materials as opposed to those which earn income by providing services.

Private annuity and charitable remainder trusts

Private annuities are contracts between two individuals to exchange a valuable asset in return for a lifetime income stream. A typical way in which this is done is the transfer of ownership in a highly valuable asset from a parent to his or her child, in return for a promise from the child to pay the parent an annuity throughout the parent's lifetime. This allows the annuitant (the parent) a lifetime income, and some of these payments are considered a return of capital and are therefore not taxable for the annuitant. However, the payments made by the child are not tax deductible to the child, and if the annuitant lives too long, the payer (child) may pay too much for the asset, transferring wealth back to the parent's estate, which may also defeat this instrument's purpose in reducing taxation at the time of the parent's death. Further, if the payer (child) dies before the annuitant (parent), it may be difficult to collect these payments without other financial instruments.

Charitable remainder trusts are another way to limit the taxation of assets as they are distributed to children, grandchildren, and other heirs. Basically, these trusts provide for the distribution of assets through annuities paid to beneficiaries (heirs), with the "remainder" held by the trust at the end of the time defined by the trust (the lifetime of the annuitants or another period) designated for ownership by a qualified charity. This limits the tax liability of beneficiaries during the time they receive distributions. As is the case with all of these instruments, the advice of a professional financial advisor is critical in the establishment of these trusts.

QTIP and Intentionally Defective Trusts

A "Qualified Terminable Interest Property" (QTIP) trust is one form of a general category of "bypass" trusts designed to provide for the income needs of a surviving spouse while also protecting assets held by the trust from federal estate taxes. The advantages of a QTIP trust lie in the fact that beneficiaries can include individuals other than the children or grand-children of a married couple. QTIP beneficiaries can include children of a prior marriage, preventing them from being cut off from their inheritance by a surviving step-parent spouse, subsequent marriage partner, or "close friend" of the surviving spouse.

An Intentionally Defective Trust is an extremely complicated in-strument that creates special circumstances for the owner of appreciating assets to transfer them to others with the least possible income tax, gift tax, and estate tax burden. Technically an "Intentionally Defective Grantor Trust" (IDGT), it defines the trust owner as the "grantor," and assigns tax liability for the trust to this individual. This tax liability is also transferred to the trust's beneficiaries. However, the assets held by an IDGT are ex-cluded from the grantor's estate, and transfers of assets into the IDGT are considered "completed" gifts by the federal government. Because this is technically treated as a "sale," it avoids taxation as a gift, and removes the asset and any appreciation from the donor's estate. IDGTs allow for other flexible management of assets held in such trusts, including the right to borrow against these funds, remove assets from the trust and exchange them for assets of equal value, or revoke the trust in favor of the grantor. Because the grantor pays the tax on trust income, the assets inside an IDGT effectively grow tax-free. The advantages an IDGT offers are the reason it is called "intentionally defective": essentially, an IDGT allows the grantor the right to take advantage of its provisions to avoid taxation and other regulations that would otherwise apply to the assets held by an IDGT.

ADVANCED FINANCIAL AND TAX PLANNING CONCEPTS

Once the basics of estate planning have been established, there may still be the need for additional work. This additional planning will be dependent on individual considerations such as cash flow and resources available to the physician and his or her family. For example, one person may have a large amount of cash investments or investments that are cash equivalent; these assets can be said to be available for immediate planning. Another person may have fewer cash accounts or liquid assets but a high amount of income from assets that cannot or should not be turned into cash—rental property and other real estate, for example. Each case requires a different approach. The investor who has more real estate as an investment may need to do more planning in terms of how the property should be owned, whether these properties should be owned in the name of a corporation, LLC, or jointly, or by one of the trusts we discussed earlier in this chapter, which may or may not need to be established.

Captive Insurance Companies

Due to the many recent changes in the health care reform and tax laws, a number of physicians have joined forces and established medical groups or even hospitals, in order to provide synergy and a uniform plan of care for patients. These groups are designed to provide more flexibility and less cost, not only to the insurance industry but also to the public. As a result of such mergers, these entities may be generating a huge level of revenue, which may also cause corresponding increases in tax liabilities. As organizations like this grow in size and complexity, risks grow to a level of scale and complexity for which there are few precedents, and the resulting cost of insuring such businesses has skyrocketed. In some cases, these premiums have become unaffordable for malpractice and other related business insurances such as workers' compensation or group medical insurance for employees. There are also other unforeseen and potentially enormous liabilities that may not be insured. In these cases, there are several opportunities and strategies that can be implemented which may not only reduce the tax liability but may also provide an adequate amount of insurance coverage for perils for which no affordable coverage exists. This form of risk management is referred to as a Captive Insurance Company. A "captive" is in fact an insurance company which the medical group or company establishes on its own, and to which it pays premiums to cover perils that currently may not be adequately insured or even insurable through traditional policies. The National Association of Insurance Commissioners (NAIC) has information regarding this sort of plan.

As can be imagined, the design and implementation of a captive insurance company is extremely complicated and needs to be the subject of a feasibility study before it can be implemented. Further, it also needs to be managed by a professional group of experts. Most tax advisors and attorneys may not be well versed in this area, and may not have enough knowledge to provide adequate recommendations or information to their clients seeking to learn more about the pros and cons of a captive. Insurance advisors, tax attorneys, and other financial professionals would need to be specifically trained and educated in this field before they would be qualified to provide this information. It's a situation that is similar to the difference between a primary care doctor and a specialist. Although the primary care doctor may have general knowledge of a broad range of conditions and health issues, only a specialist can provide treatment and diagnosis for the very narrow range of diseases and conditions grouped under their medical specialty. The primary care physician takes on the role of establishing a relationship with the patient, getting to know the patient's health status in a thorough and even detailed way, and keeping a historical record of the care the patient needs, how that care is provided, and how the patient responds to treatment. The primary care doctor can make diagnoses that may lead to treatments he or she can provide, or, in some cases, these diagnoses will call for intervention by a specialist to either administer further diagnosis tests, or to treat health issues the primary care doctor is not qualified to provide. Surgery, behavioral health services, or any number of clinical specialties such as OB/GYN services, or podiatry, are examples of these specialty care providers a primary care doctor may call in to help keep his or her patients healthy.

To continue this analogy, a professional financial advisor can provide clients with a broad overview of the concepts, resources, and tools that can be applied in the development of a solid financial plan. This advisor can also diagnose problems, troubleshoot, and in many cases provide planning services and advice to smooth out the rough spots in a client's financial plan. But when the professional services needed aren't among the advisor's skill set, he or she will add specialists like tax advisors, insurance experts, or even business management consultants to the team in order to keep a client's financial plan on track.

Premium financing and executive benefits

In some cases, individuals with high net worth or large annual incomes may have a need for similarly high amounts of life insurance, which will require high premiums. In these cases, in lieu of paying high premiums out of pocket, it may be possible to arrange for a "special" funding source in which a lending institution will make arrangements for loans to the insured. Based on the amount of these loans, the lending institution will make a portion of the policy's premium payments, while the insured pays the interest. This allows such clients to keep their cash in order to invest in their business, while they are insured with lower out of pocket premium payments. This is extremely complicated and there are risks involved. It is particularly important for clients to beware of insurance agents who present these plans as having zero cost to the client, or who represent these plans as having no interest or other payments associated with them. As financial planners, insurance companies, lending institutions, and other individuals and corporations continue to innovate and provide new options for physicians and other business people, there are also scam artists who unfortunately may be equally good at innovating for their own purposes. The key to being able to evaluate the life insurance described here is the exit strategy. Knowing when and how to pay back the loan to the lending institution, and what risks are involved in the timing of these payments, are critical elements of these plans. Again, by all means, engage a team of qualified financial advisors, insurance experts, and reputable business partners when considering these products.

Other advanced planning techniques may include setting up a defined benefit pension plan. These plans are designed to allow larger tax deductions for the doctor, and in some cases (unlike defined contribution plans which have much lower limits), defined benefit plans can allow for retirement plan contributions that may exceed several hundred thousand dollars. Defined benefit plans are very complicated and must be administered by highly qualified pension administrators and financial advisors who truly understand how to manage these assets and how to set them up properly.

CONCLUSION

I TRULY BELIEVE THAT THE IDEA behind this book is to let our clients—physicians, who are also small business owners and family members—know that they really need to have a strong financial plan in order to be successful and live the lives they envision for themselves and their families. Once such a plan is in place, it is not terribly difficult to maintain: sometimes, all that is required is to spend a few minutes every quarter to review the plan, or to take a more thorough look at least once a year to see where they are, where they need to be, and what new or familiar risks may need to be addressed through modifications to the plan. The bottom line is to make sure they have a plan to accumulate wealth while also protecting that wealth as it grows.

But physicians need to have guarantees in place to ensure that their plans are going to actually be executed. They need to stay on course with the plan that they design with the support of their team of advisors. Staying the course is the guarantee we believe is the result of the design and implementation of a sound financial plan. And that plan must be personalized to fit the circumstances of the physician's medical practice, the small business he or she owns or manages, and the family who shares his or her life away from work. A plan based on hypotheticals and if's alone is rarely the best way to go.

Traditionally, most financial planners have relied on formulaic criteria, using an estimated rate of return, along with a whole array of assumptions that make it appear their plans are "customized." But after so many years in this business, we have seen that many of these assumptions are not even close to being on track, because they either simply don't fit the individual needs of the clients they serve, or they are too rigid in their reliance on formulas and assumptions. All it takes is a few stock market crashes, or an unexpected expense, a divorce, or perhaps one or two emergency-related business expenses to completely undo their whole planning process.

Our belief is to begin with an honest assessment of the client's (in this case, the physician's) life goals, to then embark on a strategy to accumulate assets in the best way possible, and then to create the "guarantees" we believe are based on sound risk management methodologies. The best ways to manage risks are these: first, to transfer them to others whenever possible, primarily through the use of insurance; second, to train oneself and one's employees to avoid activities that increase risk and to focus on business practices that minimize them; and third, to always have a "Plan B" in the event of an unexpected crisis. In addition to all of this, there is of course our last and best advice: do not listen to people who are not trained or experienced in financial management, insurance products, or planning in general. Rely on professionals. We exist for a reason. And we can help.

www.ingramcontent.com/pod-product-compliance
Lightning Source LLC
Chambersburg PA
CBHW052013230326
41598CB00078B/3214